SOLVING THE ASSISTANT PRINCIPAL'S PUZZLE

Douglas L. Hartley, Ph.D.

EYE ON EDUCATION
6 DEPOT WAY WEST, SUITE 106
LARCHMONT, NY 10538
(914) 833–0551
(914) 833–0761 fax
www.eyeoneducation.com

Library of Congress Cataloging-in-Publication Data

Hartley, Douglas L.
  Solving the assistant principal's puzzle / Douglas L. Hartley.
    p. cm.
  ISBN 978-1-59667-120-1
  1. Assistant school principals—United States. I. Title.
  LB2831.92.H375 2009

  371.2'012—dc22

                                                    2008055576

10 9 8 7 6 5 4 3 2 1

Also Available from
EYE ON EDUCATION

The Principalship from A to Z
Ronald Williamson and Barbara R. Blackburn

Get Organized!
Time Management for School Leaders
Frank Buck

Motivating & Inspiring Teachers: The Educational
Leader's Guide for Building Staff Morale, Second Edition
Todd Whitaker, Beth Whitaker, and Dale Lumpa

Lead Me—I Dare You!
Sherrel Bergman and Judith Brough

Applying Servant Leadership in Today's Schools
Mary K. Culver

Managing Conflict: 50 Strategies for School Leaders
Stacey Edmonson, Julie Combs, and Sandra Harris

What Successful Principals Do! 169 Tips for Principals
Franzy Fleck

Professional Learning Communities:
An Implementation Guide and Toolkit
Kathleen A. Foord and Jean M. Haar

People First! The School Leader's Guide to
Building and Cultivating Relationships with Teachers
Jennifer Hindman, Angela Seiders, and Leslie Grant

Dealing with Difficult Parents
(And with Parents in Difficult Situations)
Todd Whitaker and Douglas Fiore

Leadership Connectors:
Six Keys to Developing Relationships in Schools
Phyllis Ann Hensley and LaVern Burmeister

The Instructional Leader's Guide to Informal
Classroom Observations, Second Edition
Sally J. Zepeda

Dedication

This book is dedicated to my beautiful wife Lee Ann and to my inspirational children, Ethan and Shea. You are my light, my hope, my world.

Acknowledgements

An undertaking of a project of this magnitude is nearly impossible to do alone. I must acknowledge the many tremendous educators whom I have had the honor to work with in my seventeen years as a teacher, coach, and assistant principal. I have learned so much from each through the years. There is no doubt that our students are in great hands and have futures full of promise and hope. I would like to offer a special thank you to my publisher, Mr. Robert Sickles, who inspired me to write and provided the motivation and encouragement that a true leader exudes. Bob, thank you for seeing my potential and for providing the avenue for which to share my knowledge and my thoughts. I also want to thank my parents, Lewis and Ann Hartley, who have always stood beside me and have always encouraged me to work hard at everything, knowing that there would be rewards for such hard work. Because of my upbringing I know that I cannot fool the man in the mirror and thus am true to myself and to others. Thank you.

About the Author

Douglas L. Hartley, Ph.D., is currently an assistant principal at Tabb High School in the York County School Division in Yorktown, Virginia. Dr. Hartley began his career as a high school science teacher and further worked with student athletes as a football, wrestling, and track coach in two of the division's high schools. He was nominated by his students to the *Who's Who Among American Teachers* for his passion of teaching and rapport with students. Dr. Hartley has served as an assistant principal in three of the division's four high schools under the direction of five different principals. He works within his school and school division to train teachers and paraeducators on academic management strategies that promote student engagement and improve student behavior.

Dr. Hartley was the sole winner of the 2007 Edgar L. Morphett award given by the National Council of Professors of Educational Administration (NCPEA) recognizing his dissertation as the most outstanding in the field of educational administration. He was recognized and provided a presentation at the NCPEA annual conference in Chicago in 2007. His dissertation was also selected as a distinguished paper by the Virginia Educational Research Association (VERA) and by the American Educational Research Association (AERA) where he was recognized and presented at both the annual state and national conferences. Dr. Hartley earned his bachelor's degree in Science from Longwood College (now Longwood University), master's degree in Education and Human Development from George Washington University, and doctoral degree in Educational Leadership and Policy Studies from the Virginia Polytechnic Institute and State University (Virginia Tech).

Contents

Foreword

I have trained aspiring administrators throughout the United States and they all ask for the same thing. With all of the anticipated stress of the job, they simply want to know how to survive the position. Dr. Douglas Hartley's book offers much more. His information, if followed, will provide readers with the requisite knowledge to not only survive, but thrive as assistant principals!

American schools are extremely complex organizations that require a *balanced and informed* approach to leadership from those placed in the position of assistant principal. I can recall no time in our recent history that the demands have been higher on schools. *No Child Left Behind* has placed an unprecedented level of accountability on educators. With these facts in mind, there is an increasing need for those successful in the position to share their wealth of knowledge and bridge the gap between theory and practice. Dr. Douglas Hartley has done just that. This book will provide readers with the nuts and bolts of the assistant principalship by offering practical recommendations to those who find themselves trying to navigate this often difficult journey.

I am excited for those of you who are about to turn the following pages. I'm overjoyed that you are seeking practical, research-based information. But, more importantly, I believe that the information in this book will ultimately impact the lives of the children you serve. At the end of the day, after all that you do, *education is about helping kids.* Congratulations! *You are on your way.*

John W. Hodge
Vice-President
Urban Learning and Leadership Center

Preface

One of the most important and challenging positions in the field of education is that of the assistant principal. Without great leadership at this position, schools struggle to have any chance of success. The job description of the assistant principal has changed and expanded over the past decade. The position, typically known for its heavily burdened managerial responsibilities, has crossed over into the instructional leadership domain. Although the traditional management responsibilities of the assistant principal have not waned, increased instructional accountability has waxed. While such instructional accountability is vital and welcomed by assistant principals, it does present a puzzle as to how to successfully complete the large number of managerial duties and to be a credible instructional leader simultaneously. Therefore, assistant principals have to carefully craft their daily schedules to allow for successful completion of the managerial duties while freeing up time to observe, collaborate, and lead instruction. This, of course, is easier said than done. This puzzle that I have observed and have discussed time after time prompted me to write this book. It is how the book came into being, and I hope that it will facilitate fellow assistant principals in solving the puzzle and seeing the compelling mission of our steadfast work.

The book provides a framework and strategies for solving the puzzle that current day assistant principals face daily. It is based on my experiences working in three different high schools under the tutelage of five different principals. This book is intended to be used as a practical tool and aid assistant principals in becoming the next generation of leaders in building better and stronger schools through sound instructional leadership strategies and genuine people skills. The book takes the reader through a continuum of thoughts, ideas, and strategies that are intended to provide the skills necessary to become a holistic and a well-rounded leader.

In Chapter 1, the puzzle of the assistant principal is clearly defined. Moving into a sustained and credible instructional

xiv   Solving the Assistant Principal's Puzzle

leadership role while successfully completing all of the managerial duties can be quite challenging and overwhelming. This chapter explains all of the problems and the pitfalls, and begins to suggest strategies. Chapter 2 addresses the changing dynamics of our schools and encourages assistant principals to move staff away from the one-size-fits-all instructional approach. We must determine and use better methods for engaging a variety of learners. This requires leadership that moves teachers out of their comfort zones. Chapter 3 talks about what the next generation of school leaders will look like. For our students and our country to be successful in a globally competitive world, we must begin to motivate and to encourage our teachers to take risks, to step outside of their comfort zones, and to find new ways of engaging all students. Chapter 4 tackles the dual role of the assistant principal and includes discussion regarding the importance of managerial and instructional duties. Both are necessary for a school to run efficiently and effectively and I address strategies to make assistant principals successful at both.

The use of power in the position is a slippery slope. Chapter 5 addresses power in such a way that it benefits leaders without making them feel awkward. Chapter 6 addresses how relationship building is a great method to get the most out of those who are led and produces a better product than that forced through power and micromanagement. Relationships are made stronger through constant and sustained collaboration and recognition. Chapter 7 addresses the need to collaborate with staff and with the principal so that the school and the assistant principal are on the same page and have the same actions. Going off in different directions does not move the team forward. Chapter 8 describes what a better and stronger school is and how to get there. We must work to improve; complacency is the enemy of improvement. Finally, extensive concluding remarks tie everything together to illustrate a picture of the completed puzzle, an opportunity to see what it all looks like when the pieces fit together. Indeed, the job offers the opportunity to have a galvanizing impact on many people and many lives, but an assistant principal has to take control, not be controlled by the many pitfalls and trappings associated with the profession of the assistant principalship.

Introduction

How did American schools get to where they are today, and how do school leaders function in this new environment to provide a quality education for all children? More specifically, how do assistant principals function in this new environment, which has placed important instructional demands upon an already heavy managerial position?

The assistant principalship is one of the most difficult positions in education, but it is also one of the most important. Without effective assistant principals, who are expected to be a jack-of-all-trades, schools quickly falter from their mission. School climates and cultures suffer, and ultimately students are negatively impacted. The assistant principalship forces the individual to be a manager and a leader, in a relationship in which there can be only one leader, the principal. This dichotomy presents a true challenge for assistant principals, but it is a worthy challenge that can be achieved or lessened in magnitude through a variety of formal and informal strategies. Developing wisdom, confidence, and knowledge through the assistant principalship is a benefit that will prepare a person to move from manager to leader. The role is to be patient and gain experience. This book is about how to gain the type of experience that is needed. This experience may help in running a school or assist in being the best assistant principal possible.

It seems that for a long period of time in the history of American public schools, a one-size-fits-all instructional approach was successful and effective. But, for whom was this system successful and effective? This one size fits all instructional approach, however, is no longer valid, and as educators are now coming to realize, no longer successful or effective in the American education arena. This is the foundation for which the concept of differentiated instruction has been built. Changes that employ strategies to meet the needs of a diverse group of learners is needed and needed now. Assistant principals have to be a part of leading this change. But, this change presents a dilemma, a puzzle for assistant principals because the heavy managerial duties have not dissolved and are perhaps increasing.

The philosophies and the practices in the field of education that were once static and stable are now fluid and changing, not easy to put hands around or to hold. Surely, the question arises as to how education has moved from a previous static state to a now fluid state. The answer is embedded in familiar pedagogical terms—higher accountability standards through the *No Child Left Behind Act* (NCLB) of 2001, and the changing student population that schools in this country now serve. Perhaps the latter is more momentous in today's society, but in tandem, the question to this fluid state undoubtedly is answered.

The challenge for beginning and aspiring assistant principals is not to manage schools effectively (which historically has been the case), but rather to meet the instructional needs of the students of today while performing all of the managerial duties that have not changed, and will not change because they still have to be performed by somebody (more on that topic later). Yes, I am saying that the managerial responsibilities side of education has remained relatively static, although steadily increasing in magnitude, throughout the history of American education. On the other hand, the instructional responsibilities are fluid and possibly even new for many assistant principals, and continue to grow in importance.

There are adjustments that have to be made to managerial duties from time to time, but the content and the intent remain the same—keep the school running effectively and efficiently so that instruction can take place. However, instructional responsibilities added on top of enormous managerial duties can be a new and overwhelming experience for novice assistant principals. It is a compounded effect in which assistant principals are pitted each day in a race against time—the school clock. New job responsibilities in the area of instruction provide great opportunities for assistant principals to prosper and to grow professionally, but must be managed carefully to provide the best educational benefit to children. Slipping in one area is bound to have an adverse effect in the other.

This is not to say that assistant principals are not good or comfortable with instruction—that is not my point. Many as-

sistant principals whom I have known were excellent classroom teachers who knew how to engage and how to motivate
all types of students while exhibiting strong academic management skills and genuine student rapport. However, their
focus, as was mine, was limited to their classroom, their content, their students, and their assessment results. Unintended
isolation from colleagues was a big part of their past, as was
mine. Their focus now as assistant principals is still on instruction, but on much broader terms, and on top of their already
stretched managerial schedules. After all, effective instruction
cannot take place without the successful completion of the
managerial needs of a school. Assistant principals who were
formerly teachers have the unique perspective of having once
been masterful in the classroom and now having the complex
global perspective of being an instructional leader plus a building manager. While instruction is and should be the backbone
of any school, the fusing of this backbone is from the successful completion of the managerial duties—the behind the scenes
work that is assumed completed and very seldom recognized,
unless it does not get done.

An assistant principal may find that the amount of time
needed to complete managerial duties can be quite overwhelming and frustrating. Assistant principals may begin to wonder
when they would even have a chance to become involved with
instruction in any capacity. This is a legitimate concern and it
may take some settling into the position before the answer becomes clear as each school is unique. Let me mention, that by
instruction, I am not referring to standard teacher observations
and year-end summative evaluations. These tend to be set at
a required number per year and may have nothing to do with
instruction if they are rushed and completed merely as an ob-
ligation without any instructional dialogue. If this is the case,
it would be just another managerial duty because it has no instructional value to the evaluator or to the teacher. Again, these
formative observation tools can have great value, but must be
used in a prescribed manner to have intended benefits. They
must be timely, include dialogue, and have the appropriate follow up for support and for clarification. Where the evaluator
can go wrong is by rushing these observations for the sake of

getting them done, which can be very tempting in such a taxing position. Techniques to commit the assistant principal to instruction and instructional leadership while accomplishing necessary managerial responsibilities are discussed throughout the book.

This book acknowledges the workload, the pressure, and the accountability placed on the person in the position of the assistant principalship yet demonstrates that instructional leadership can be accomplished in an uplifting and motivating manner. This is very important because assistant principals need the positive and uplifting exposure that comes with instruction to pull them out of the negative rut that can come with an overexposure to managerial duties (e.g., discipline, parental complaints, and specific special education issues). There is no doubt as to the seemingly endless frustration that can occur in the role of assistant principal, but in this book an emphasis is placed on the positive and on the importance of prevailing in such pivotal educational times to help to build a better and a stronger school. This book recognizes the hard work required to be an effective assistant principal and acknowledges that even with the implementation of the advice given in this book, the job will at times seem insurmountable, but the reward for the effort to succeed is priceless.

It is not my intent or the intent of this book to present the specifics of how to do things as an assistant principal, but what to consider and what to expect. The how varies from school to school and principal to principal. It further varies with school board and superintendent goals and initiatives, which are generally carried out by assistant superintendents, directors, instructional specialists, curriculum assistants, and other relevant positions at the school board office down to principals. When I feel that it is appropriate and meaningful, I do make some suggestions that I believe are helpful or provide key words or topics that can be researched and applied to any unique situation. The book does provide insight on what to do as an assistant principal and what needs to be done while moving from manager to leader in one of the toughest jobs in the field of education. This book is practical in nature and provides ideas, tips, and examples that will hopefully give fulfillment to an often unrecognized position—the assistant principalship.

1

The Assistant Principalship's Puzzle

A puzzle is a problem presented to a person that is difficult to solve or a situation difficult to resolve and to be unsure as to action or choice (Webster, 1983). Such a dilemma may require guesswork or experimentation to find the best or most appropriate solution. So, what does this have to do with being an assistant principal? A brief look at the job description for an assistant principal has the word *puzzle* written (metaphorically) all over it. The assistant principal's puzzle is this: How do I successfully complete the enormous managerial demands of the job while becoming a credible instructional leader and without stealing the principal's thunder? Not an easy task!

Credible Instructional Leadership

I added the word *credible* before instructional leader because I am referring to the type of instructional leadership that will be widely trusted, accepted, and sustained in a particular school that is striving to become better and stronger. Merely performing some obligatory staff development on occasion may be considered instructional leadership, and some of it may very well be, but it is not credible instructional leadership if teachers never intend to use it after they leave the training and the administrator never gets a chance to follow up on the training provided to see to its implementation. This is merely a waste of time for everybody involved, time that may have been better used elsewhere or in some other capacity.

Instructional leadership takes many hours of research, visiting classrooms, collaborating with teachers and colleagues, and looking internally for the best practices that can be used school-wide. The key to staff buy-in for instructional change is not that the administration says it works, or the research says it works, or a speaker at a conference says it works, but that there are authentic examples of where it has worked in the building with students and with teachers—and they say it works! This is what teachers really want to see because they will quickly say that instructional strategies from outsiders may work elsewhere, but not at this school.

Finding Talent From Within

It is not to say that there are not terrific strategies generated from the outside that can be modified and applied or that there are not good professional developers who can help schools with sound instructional strategies. It is, however, to say that teachers, in my experience, are more likely to accept and to use strategies that have been proven in their own school with their own students by their own colleagues to whom they can go for support and for clarification as they enter into new, unpredictable waters. I have brought in outside staff developers who were wonderful and may even have been needed to light a spark. But they do eventually leave, and that is when the school has to turn to its internal talent to keep the torch lit.

Teachers are more comfortable with their own because of familiarity and accessibility, which is not always afforded by outside professional developers. Once outsiders give their training, they leave and usually do not come back, unless prearranged to do so. Implementing strategies from the outside works best when the trainer can be around for a sustained period of time to provide clarity during the implementation process (the most critical part), which is usually very rare and very expensive for schools. Additionally, the school is at the mercy of the trainer regarding followup dates and further training, which can result in large gaps of time wherein strategies can be implemented incorrectly or not at all because of a lack of clarity. Adding the new teachers joining the staff who were not part of previous training sessions leaves the administration with many holes to fill. These holes can be better filled from the inside than from the outside. This filling of the holes improves instruction within the school and reinforces the mission of building a better and a stronger school. It allows for new teachers to immediately begin as part of a collaborative team and to start using best practices that other teachers are already successfully using. Again, it is not my intention to discourage outside help, but to encourage a school to use its internal talent. Sometimes it does take outside help to light the flame and I use these valuable resources to improve the internal talent.

Increased Responsibility

We know that in today's schools the principal is the number one instructional leader and is held accountable for such by many people, most notably the superintendent, the school board, and the parents. Certainly, this is no secret in this era of American public education. The emphasis for principals in the past decade, but especially since and because of the implementation of the *No Child Left Behind Act* (NCLB, 2001), has shifted to student achievement, thereby evolving the principal into an instructional leader rather than a building manager. Although the guidelines of the NCLB legislation continue to be a hot-bed issue (e.g., funding and benchmark issues) among the states, the intent of the law is hard to argue or to criticize.

Goertz and Duffy (2001) reported that every state has responded to NCLB by implementing some type of assessment and accountability, which falls on the principal. Hess (2003) noted that the traditional responsibilities of the principal have not disappeared, but the focus is now on using data and research to drive instructional decisions. This is not a bad thing—actually, it is quite a good thing for children—but it is a crucial beginning point for this book as it is where the explanation of the evolution of the assistant principal's puzzle—balancing instructional leadership with heavily saturated managerial duties—begins.

McGuire (2002) supported this claim of increased responsibility based on a year-long study of school administrators in Michigan. She reported that the position of a principal in Michigan has expanded into nine layers of duties requiring expertise. These duties are curriculum; grant writing; school law; marketing and public relations; diplomacy with parents and community; security and safety; special education; education administration; and building management. Although these duties have always fallen under the umbrella of the principalship, they are increasing in magnitude concurrently with student achievement accountability. Keep in mind that this was in 2002, so the magnitude now may be even greater.

Keeping the Focus on Instruction

The assistant principal will need to absorb some or many of these duties (mentioned above) to permit the principal freedom to be a true instructional leader. But, the assistant principal has to be careful about being buried under these duties and losing his or her instructional focus of improving teaching and learning. Nonetheless, the puzzle has evolved over time and will continue to expand without any salient changes to the current educational structure. Some states are beginning to look into organizational structures to address this domino effect, which will be discussed later. As the puzzle evolves, so does the need for adaptation by the assistant principal. Without adapting to this new environment, the assistant principal will quickly perish in the managerial quagmire and become extinct. Of course, I am talking about the person, not the position.

Of more interest, in my experiences, is that many parent complaints about school issues are primarily about managerial issues (e.g., parking, buses, lunch periods, lockers, athletics, and activities), with only a few complaints truly dealing with instruction. Even when grievances initially appear to be about instruction, they actually tend to be about grade disputes and grading practices, not really about the delivery of instruction or the curriculum. These managerial issues usually come to the assistant principal via phone calls or emails during the hours of instruction, forcing a decision on how to prioritize time. Do I address the issue now or do I wait because I need to get into the classrooms? Although the answer seems obvious, it is not. It is actually multifaceted and complex, often leaving assistant principals in a lose–lose situation.

The job requires keeping issues off the principal's desk, which may at times pull the assistant principal from instruction. Parents may decide that because an issue has not been taken care of immediately that appearing in person (thus creating an additional problem) may speed up the process or that by calling the central office things will happen more quickly. When parents are upset or frustrated, they, sometimes understandably, tend to forget that their child is not the only one in the school. The best thing to do is to first weigh the situation for how quickly it needs to be attended to and, second, no matter what is decided as far as priority, always call the parent to acknowledge the concern and give an approximate time frame for when the issue will be addressed. Just be sure that this promise is fulfilled.

Brief phone calls give parents the opportunity to vent and to feel like they have been heard. Most of the time this works because the parent is not left stewing or speculating as to why a message has not been returned or resolved. Remember that some issues have to be addressed while students are in the building and accessible for due process and questioning. I later strongly express the importance of relationship building, and I believe this is a start with parents, who fan the community fires and thus the reputation for building credibility. Because the tide can rise very quickly, taking a few minutes to acknowledge a concern can buy many hours in the long run, preventing problems from becoming exacerbated.

Becoming an Instructional Leader

With all of the talk about instructional leadership, an important question now surfaces. How do I serve as an instructional leader without stealing the principal's thunder or stepping on the principal's toes? After all, we have learned that instructional leadership has been placed squarely on the shoulders of the principal and we know that many duties of an assistant principal are management related, but not all! There are a couple of answers to solving this puzzle and thus a couple of chapters dedicated to these answers. First, the assistant principal has to prove to the principal that he or she can stay afloat with primary management responsibilities while moving into instructional waters. Second, the assistant principal has to prove to the principal that he or she is dedicated to school improvement through systemic enhancements in instruction. This may be demonstrated in a variety of ways such as researching current successful instructional practices, attending conferences, working with instructional teams, and training staff during professional development opportunities. Finally, the assistant principal has to collaborate with the principal so that he or she is working as a team and not outside the parameters of the mission that the principal has set for the school.

Going off and doing things alone may show initiative, but not when it is done outside of the scope of the principal. This may be considered as stealing the thunder or stepping on the toes of the principal. Discuss with the principal the role of the assistant principal with instruction and what skills are being brought to the table. Principals are more than happy to carve out a leadership role, so be sure to discuss what that role is. Showing initiative by presenting personal ideas that support the principal's goals and vision will help the assistant principal achieve an instructional leadership role.

The principal may be the team captain, but the assistant principal is a valuable teammate. However, do not go off alone without discussing it first with the principal. This may be misinterpreted and also may not be part of the principal's vision. This may lead to the principal questioning motives, which is not in the assistant principal's best interest. It is kind of like the quarterback changing the coach's play in the huddle. Let the principal serve as the compass for choosing what direction to take with instructional leadership and then do the very best to get the principal to that destination.

The key is taking things a little bit at a time and building confidence to move on to bigger and better instructional opportunities. Proceed slowly and with caution so that it is done correctly and so that the managerial duties are not neglected. Because of the many responsibilities it is a good idea to keep track on a weekly basis of tasks completed, so if something is left unfulfilled, time on other tasks can be justified. All of the topics discussed in this chapter are addressed individually and more specifically throughout the remaining chapters of the book.

2

The Changing
Dynamic of Schools

In most cases, assistant principals will find that their school is not like the school that their grandparents, parents, or even the one they themselves once attended. If one is working in a homogeneous setting, things are still different. By this, I mean that thanks to major improvements in technology, the global competitive playing field is becoming leveled and thus schools need to prepare students for such a competitive world. Thomas Friedman (2005), author of *The World Is Flat*, said,

> Clearly, it is now possible for more people than ever to collaborate and compete in real time with more other people on more different kinds of work from more different corners of the planet and on a more equal footing than at any previous time in the history of the world—using computers, email, networks, teleconferencing, and dynamic new software. (p. 8)

This flattening has changed the dynamics of America's schools along with high stakes testing and accountability. In many cases, the students have changed as well, and in a variety of ways. It seems that students born and raised in the technology age may need more interactivity, more stimuli, more grouping. The original design of schools that was based on homogeneity has changed. Just think about it, on many older school buildings there are still the words "boys" and "girls" etched in stone above the main entrances as to what side of the building students were to enter for their lessons. Because we now work in more heterogeneous schools, we need to recognize that the instructional practices we have employed in the past may not work for our current and future students, at least not for all or many of them. Even in rare cases where the students have not drastically changed, the need for improved instructional practices is evident for the competitive future of students and the generational transformations that have occurred within these students.

Factors Influencing Change

With more diverse classrooms, special education inclusion models, limited English proficient students, and students who are used to constant interaction and stimuli (associated with modern technology), an examination of how we deliver knowledge to our students is absolutely necessary and vital. A final piece to the change in dynamics is that schools are a reflection of society. Drugs, violence, gangs, and family issues creep into the schoolhouse walls. Although the reflection of society has always been true of schools, it can be argued that these problems have substantially increased with time and impact students who are much younger than in past decades. Easy access to destructive information and toxic resources has further exacerbated this problem and relief from such issues seems to be far on the horizon, if at all. Therefore, administrators have to understand that while we cannot control the product, we can control the process—how we teach students.

Fixing the Factors

A combination of the aforementioned has drastically changed the dynamics of schools. Interestingly, these forces at work are all different from one another, but require the same fix, although this is not an overnight fix. This fix has to start with strong instructional leadership from more than just the principal. It requires teachers to reflect on their current instructional practices, take risks, and then make continuous improvements. It requires collaboration among all stakeholders to build a better and a stronger school—a school in which students and staff look forward to coming each day because each day presents an applicable learning challenge in a safe and welcoming environment. This fix requires that everybody involved in the education of children understands what is at stake and takes action. It requires parents to do their part and to take ownership in supporting their child's education. Despite the present-day erosion of the family unit, parents can still be an important, influential, and inspiring role in a child's education and life. Remember that global competition is already here and eventually will be knocking in record numbers on everyone's door. Will our children be prepared? We better hope so!

The instructional leadership component of this fix may look very different for the assistant principal than for the principal. Typically, the principal will create the vision for where the he or she wants the school to go or to be by a stated period of time. The principal may map this out along with how the school is going to get there over time—who will do what and when. Benchmarks will be created and reviewing data from those benchmarks will determine if the school continues along the original road map or needs to take an alternate route. No path to a vision should be set in stone, only the vision itself because it is the compass.

A Team Effort

Jim Collins (2001), in *Good to Great*, said "Great vision without great people is irrelevant" (p. 42). Thus the principal has to have great people, a team, beside him or her and these people are the assistant principal and the teachers. However, it cannot stop here either. "Great people" refers to many people in a building who can have an impact on a child in any way, shape, or form. The daytime custodian is very popular among students at my school because he has a way of making them feel welcome and wanted. We need all adults in the building to be able to relate to children in such a way.

The assistant principal may be responsible for all of the same things as the principal, depending on how the principal has assigned the necessary roles within a school. If this is the case, it is a good thing, even though it may seem like a great deal of work (which it is). If the assistant principal finds himself or herself primarily or only assigned to managerial duties, it is time for a change. The assistant principal should ask that some instructional duties be added to his or her responsibilities.

Notice, I did not say to give up anything, but simply to ask for some instructional leadership opportunities. Giving up something may mean passing it on to someone else. That is not good leadership unless there is some way that it benefits the recipient. Delegating is a leadership trait, but there can be a fine line between delegating and dumping. Examine everything that is delegated to ensure it has a benefit to the recipient.

Ultimately, the principal is in charge of student achievement; therefore, the pressure is greater and the principal may see instruction through a different set of lenses than those of the assistant principal. This does not mean that one set of lenses is better than the other, just that they are different. This statement is not meant to minimize the instructional role of the assistant principal, but to understand that the role may be to support the principal's vision of good instruction, not create that vision. The principal's vision may not be the assistant principal's vision (although it could be), but it needs to be supported faithfully.

Giving the Vision Time

This idea of good instruction may differ slightly between the principal and the assistant principal, but it is the principal who carries the ultimate responsibility at the end of the day. Therefore, assistant principals, if they want a piece of the instructional pie, will collaborate with the principal to do what is in the best interest of students. An assistant principal can learn from the principal by putting together the pieces of the instructional puzzle over time. It takes time to form and to implement an effective instructional vision and plan, perhaps three to five years. Good instruction does not happen overnight, but as assistant principals who are heavily burdened with managerial duties that often do have "quick fixes," we may look for the same with instruction—bad idea! By "quick fixes" I am referring to those invariable managerial duties that are burdensome, but can be completed rather quickly because they become automatic.

Instruction takes many years of development, refinement, and improvement to become great instruction. This does not mean that good things are not happening in classrooms now. With appropriate professional development, coaching, and collaboration, teachers can have an almost immediate positive impact on students. However, these teachers will reflect, refine, and improve each year and become better and better with time. Indeed, experience will be a teacher to all who are stepping out of their comfort zones to find new ways to engage and to reach their students. Following these suggestions will give assistant principals a chance to become involved with instruction and gain valuable leadership experience under the tutelage of the principal.

3

The Next Generation of Leaders

From the time the tardy bell rings in the morning until the dismissal bells rings in the late afternoon, administrators are in the classrooms, interacting with students, and collaborating with teachers. At the end of the day it is off to meet with professional learning teams or to discuss collaboratively with teachers in small groups what has been observed throughout the week in classrooms and what they have been seeing and doing. Collaborative brainstorming sessions quickly lead to potential strategies to identified problems. Reviewing assessments and discussing data in teams along with mapping out the next steps are a natural part of the administrators' after school activities. Paperwork and managerial duties have been minimized or designated to others (remember to designate not to dump) so that administrators can focus on instructional leadership while addressing minimal paperwork loads which only they can oversee and sign. This is an ideal day for an administrator who is instructionally driven.

Equal and Prompt Attention to Instruction

In many cases the idea day is still not a reality for assistant principals. Indeed, the author of *Results Now* (2006), Mike Schmoker, explains:

For decades, "compliance" has allowed schools to be busily occupied with "change" without achieving improvement. These policies have promoted fragmentation rather than focus, and ambiguity where clarity was desperately needed. This has given us schools that meet every bureaucratic requirement while failing to provide a viable curriculum and effective instruction, thus guaranteeing boredom, frustration, and the failure of students by tens of millions. (p. 158)

It is obvious from this Schmoker quote and from the information that I have shared thus far, that many obstacles exist that can derail an administrator off the track of an ideal day of being an instructional leader. Schmoker shares that instruction takes a back seat to managerial assignments and bureaucratic requirements, and that perhaps if instruction were tied to deadlines, dates, and required paperwork, it would receive equal and prompt consideration. Ultimately, somebody has to carry out these bureaucratic requirements, and because nothing much has changed in the bureaucratic structure, it falls predominately on the shoulders of the assistant principal.

This is fine for now, because hopefully, the individual knew what an assistant principal does before applying for the position, and thus should not be too surprised or disappointed by the expectations. I say too surprised because this job is full of surprises and one just never knows what will turn up next. I learn something new all the time, sometimes every day. What is not appropriate is to let the bureaucratic requirements derail the mission of instructional leadership, which is visiting classrooms everyday, collaborating, and giving praise and feedback to teachers. Some days derailment will happen. Just do not let all the trains jump off the track.

Keeping a Sense of Purpose

While instruction is a long and hard trip, there can still be rest stops, breaks, along the way to make the trip more fun and more refreshing. Such reflection recharges the batteries for the next stage of the journey. Mike Schmoker (2006) is a big proponent of celebrating "small successes" because waiting until the end to recognize major accomplishments could be too late. People have already faded or dropped out of the race because there was no desire left, no motivation to continue—hopelessness.

Phillip C. Schlechty (2002), in *Working on the Work: An Action Plan for Teachers, Principals, and Superintendents*, stated:

The key to the survival of public education in America is the development of a cadre of school leaders who have a clear grasp of the purpose of schools: ensuring that every child, every day, is provided with engaging work to do that results in the child's learning something that is important to the child and to the continuation of the culture. Leaders also must be skilled in creating the conditions in the systems they lead (schools and school districts) that support the changes needed to enable the schools to serve their purpose. (p. 52–53)

It is clear that a new generation of leadership is needed for not only the survival of public education in America, but also for the survival of America as it competes in the knowledge age in this globally competitive world. For our future and the future of our children, school leaders must begin to create a culture that fosters student engagement and results in learning that develops future competitive citizens. The key is to establish and sustain a strong instructional focus. Indeed, a new generation of leadership is needed to enable schools to fulfill this purpose. This leadership must begin now and it must begin with the next generation of leaders.

Understanding the Next Generation of Leadership

To become the next generation of leader, a person must have a clear understanding as to what leadership is. Stephen R. Covey (2004) described leadership as follows: "Leadership is communicating to people their worth and potential so clearly that they come to see it themselves" (p. 98). Covey tells us that this is the kind of leadership that influences and endures. Although some might claim that this has always been the definition of leadership, I would argue that now more than ever leaders will be asking people to step outside of their comfort zones. This will require a whole new level and a whole new type of leadership, which involves less management and more motivation and more coaching. According to Jim Collins (2001), this type of leadership is known as level five "executive leadership," which he believes "[b]uilds enduring greatness through a paradoxical blend of personal humility and professional will" (p. 20). It is not that a level five leader does not have personal ambitions or an ego, but that the institutional goals are placed ahead of individual goals. If the leader cannot do this, there should be no expectation that his or her followers will do it. If the followers do not do it, there is no chance that the organization will prosper and thrive. Covey informs us of what is known as the "leadership challenge," which is what the next generation of leaders will face:

> The highest challenge inside organizations, including families, is to set them up and run them in a way that enables each person to inwardly sense his or her innate worth and potential for greatness and to contribute his or her unique talents and passion—in other words, voice—to accomplish the organization's purpose and highest priorities in a principle-centered way. We could call this the *Leadership Challenge*. (p. 99)

Assistant principals must be ready and willing to meet this challenge and to bring out the innate worth of all people led. This is the next generation of leadership.

4

The Dual Role of the Assistant Principal

Almost every job, task, or problem in a school building has or may have some tie to the assistant principal. New assistant principals may have a general idea as to what the position requires and perhaps what to expect. They have either watched their previous assistant principals closely, spoken with them about their duties, worked in an internship position, or have studied the position requirements closely. Despite all of these efforts, no one really knows the specifics of the job until they actually perform it. Duties and assignments vary from school to school and from principal to principal. There are many on-the-job experiences that shape and mold an assistant principal. These experiences should be used as opportunities to learn and to grow professionally. The more experiences a person has, the better the person can be as a leader.

There is no training like on-the-job training. Interestingly, while experience is gained each and every day, no two issues are exactly the same, and thus a foundation of knowledge is built over time, but mastery remains relatively elusive. This is why relationship building (discussed in Chapter 6) is so important for assistant principals. The more people a person turns to for answers or suggestions based on their experiences and knowledge, the more the individual is able to make the appropriate and best possible decisions for each unique situation. Departing into unfamiliar territory alone can place the assistant principal in a bad situation. Making controversial decisions alone can be worse. Regardless of the duty that the assistant principal is undertaking, it can be divided into managerial or instructional. These duties are discussed in detail in the following sections.

Managerial duties and their importance are discussed first followed by instructional duties and their importance.

The Managerial Role

How important is it?

As I mentioned earlier, failing to do managerial duties will, perhaps, end an assistant principal's tenure. That is how important managerial duties are to a school (see the Appendix for a list of managerial duties). The assistant principal has duties that were created and designed to enable a school to run effectively and efficiently and must be performed successfully. There is no flexibility. It just has to be done. The principal does not have the time to micromanage managerial duties or to fret over their completion. Remember, the assistant principal is next in line behind the principal and must act accordingly. If the assistant principal cannot show the principal that he or she can responsibly do the things that impact students indirectly (managerial responsibilities), the principal will never have the confidence to give the assistant principal the reigns to those things that impact students directly—namely, instruction. Therefore, it is wise to develop good time-management skills to maximize each day for the successful completion of all assigned duties.

Proactive Problem Solving

The assistant principal has to realize that there are only so many hours in a day, and that there are commitments outside the schoolhouse walls (yes, administrators can have personal lives). With this said the assistant principal has to be very organized and prepared to attack certain duties before they ever become due. If a person waits for a due date and then issues unexpectedly pop up (e.g., fight, bus accident, special education issues, drug search, or family illness), he or she is more likely to miss the due date or push the limit on completion, resulting in a lack of confidence by the principal or even by others further up the chain of command. Accidents do occasionally happen, but being repetitive in missing deadlines will not be forgiven.

An assistant principal must always remember that the happenings in a school usually will not match his or her "to do" list or daily planner. There is no control over this. Good administrators anticipate problems and prioritize their schedules so that unexpected interruptions minimally impact instructional goals. They may have an effect for a day or two, but not for the week or month. Good administrators are flexible enough to make changes as incidents occur. Good administrators may not be happy about it (I never am), but should be organized enough and have enough flexibility built into the schedule to account for unexpected problems. This is easier said than done and I emphasize the importance of tackling due dates rather than waiting to be tackled by them. A teacher in my school has a poster that states, "WARNING: Due dates are closer than they appear." I strongly recommend keeping that quote in mind when developing time management techniques.

Taking Pride in the Managerial Role

I would be remiss if I did not address how important the managerial role is in educating children. It is not my intent in this book to minimize this part of the job. I take great pride in this aspect of leadership and its importance to the school. Indeed, proper management of a school allows and can perhaps determine how effective instruction is in the school building. There are some who would argue that if there is effective instruction in the school, everything else will take care of itself. This is a good point, especially when it comes to preventing discipline problems via student engagement. However, it cannot stand in isolation as other events occur outside the classroom and outside the scope of great teaching that can impact instruction. Therefore, good instruction by itself is not enough to take care of everything that needs to be attended to in a school. There is also a need for strong management skills from the assistant principal. Just do not let it be the defining area of leadership.

Although I sincerely believe that instruction is the "meat and potatoes" of education, teachers who deliver that instruction must be able to do it under ideal conditions. This instruction must be to students who arrive for class on time, do not disrupt others, are not hungry, and are not afraid to be at school because of bullying, harassment, gangs, drug pushers, and other related concerns. Because there are so many variables that can have an effect on learning and the learning environment, it is essential that assistant principals stay on top of their managerial duties. Unfortunately, these duties often overlap, conflict, and sometimes overtake instruction, producing the puzzle. This puzzle has no immediate solution beyond structural changes and hard work, but there are strategies throughout this book that make it more controllable for an assistant principal.

The savvy administrator will anticipate problems and plan accordingly, but even the best planned day can fall victim to certain unexpected problems—when it rains, it pours. Problems that are newsworthy and can affect the safety of students and staff will require immediate attention and subsequent action along with many hours of paperwork and public rapport. These problems require immediate attention and subconsciously shift instruction to the back burner. However, I encourage assistant principals to plan to go into each school day with instruction as their first priority and then play the hand that is dealt as the day unfolds. At least set aside a chunk of the day for instruction if all else fails.

Managing All of the Responsibilities

The single most important question for an assistant principal is how do I manage to get all of my duties accomplished as well as fulfill my role as an instructional leader in my school building? I wish I could give an easy answer, and perhaps if I could I would solve some of the turnover issues, stress, and burnout experienced at this level of leadership. On the other hand, I can give an honest answer, which unfortunately includes working no fewer hours, but prioritizing and adjusting the schedule to meet particular needs. Realizing that we do have a life outside of our careers, the problem becomes even more complex. Working longer hours would not be the solution, regardless of commitments outside school. By this I mean that one will still work many hours at this position, but there is a point of diminishing returns when overdoing it. Being at work physically, but absent mentally severely diminishes one's work capacity. Unfortunately, this effect seems to occur while students are in the building and assistant principals need to be at their best (e.g., the morning following a late night ball game which did not allow time at home between school and the game). Late nights followed by early mornings can have a compounding effect with time.

Working fewer hours is not the answer either because the job does not lend itself to such a privilege. I would suggest that a beginning assistant principal evaluate what he or she wants their home life to be and work from this point. By this, I mean the quality of time spent at home as opposed to the amount of time spent at home. There is a big difference. Lying on the couch in front of the television and not interacting with family is not quality time, although from time to time it can be relaxing and refreshing. *Caution:* School administration is a job that can suck a person in very quickly because there is a sense of relief for getting things accomplished when nobody is in the building to distract the assistant principal. Be aware of this so as to avoid living at the school. From time to time it can be beneficial, but if it becomes a habit, it is relied on as extra time. This means something has to give. I address this as I proceed through the chapter.

I have found that getting up half an hour earlier (if at all possible) and getting to the office earlier allows me some extra time to complete some managerial duties as well as to prepare for the day ahead of me. Typically, this uninterrupted time for me is a chance for reflection and mental preparation for the day that awaits me. Additionally, if there are any problems (e.g., power outage) that occurred overnight, I have time to react to them rather than be blindsided by them, so that the school day can operate as normally as possible. Typically, this is a time that my family is sleeping and the time I gain while they are sleeping may be used at the end of the day when they are home and want to play or have activities that I need to attend. Remember what I said earlier about quantity versus quality of family time. An assistant principal has to find ways to create quality personal time.

Integrating Family Into the Job

I enjoy taking my children to ball games and extracurricular events for which I am assigned supervision. This gives us a chance to spend time together and exposes my children to a variety of positive activities that they one day may want to do. This is what I call "integrating family into the job." Think about it this way: This is quality time that I get to spend with my children while exposing them to positive extracurricular activities. A word of advice: When taking children to ball games, bring a few extra dollars. Children love the concession stand and it helps keep them quiet and supports the athletic programs. Just bear in mind that a contingency plan such as an office (safe place) or an adult that the children can go with in case of a fight or issue may be required.

Game coverage allows me time to pop in the office to complete a few things (e.g., emails, voicemails, and paperwork), especially if it is a small crowd on that particular night. Events such as formal dances and school musicals are an opportunity to take a spouse out for an evening and time can be spent together by first going to dinner and then by keeping each other company at the event. These are not perfect solutions by any means, but it is reality in the world of school leadership. I try to make things work by integrating my family into school events and to make it a positive and fun experience for all. This seems to be quite successful and I sometimes find myself going to games that I am not scheduled to supervise, but find it to be positive entertainment for the whole family. Students also get to see administrators in a different, more laid back perspective, perhaps in a pair of jeans and a school color tee-shirt. The only catch is duty might call should something happen during the game or event when attending for the fun of it. Building relationships is so important, especially with students. Going to extracurricular events is a good and fun way to do this.

Working Outside the Office

The idea of taking work home and doing some work on the weekends does not sit well with me, but I have found that just by dedicating thirty minutes an evening and an hour or two on the weekends really helps take away the anxiety of the next day and keeps my head above the "administrivia" waters. Being prepared, especially after weekends, really makes the next day easier. Also, some individuals may wish to go back to school to work on a doctorate degree or some type of advanced degree, which will have an impact on time management and will stretch personal time even further. This undertaking requires a personal and family commitment and as my family decided before I began the doctoral degree process, it would be an investment and a sacrifice that would have positive long-term dividends. This did require many hours away from home, including a summer residency requirement, but now that I am finished I am trying to make it up to my family. They attended my graduation and got to experience a large college campus and all of its offerings. As a result of completing my doctorate, my children will one day have an example of hard work and dedication to follow for achieving their dreams and their aspirations.

I was about a year and a half into my assistant principalship before I began working on my doctorate. This allowed me time to become familiar with the job before I put too much on my plate at one time. In reflection, I am glad that I heeded the advice of others to wait as I would have been completely overwhelmed by the demands of the job and doctoral-level course work (let alone the dissertation process). Some school districts may pay for some or all of a doctoral program through a tuition reimbursement plan, which can make getting started very tempting. Take time and do what is comfortable.

So Many Different Duties

The number of managerial duties that an assistant principal will face in a career is too great in length to discuss each one in detail. However, there are some major duties that I will point out because of their significance. These duties may be discussed because of their importance or because of their time consumption. Both of these are important factors in planning a schedule as an assistant principal. What I do not cover in discussion throughout this book is included in list format in the Appendix. It is important that I mention everything that I have been exposed to in order to present an array of duties. The Appendix includes many duties, but probably not all that an assistant principal is exposed to while on the job. These vary based on the individual school and the principal charged with running that school. Furthermore, it does not include the fires that pop up during the school day that must be put out before things get worse, which can be arduous. However, it is a fairly inclusive list (in alphabetical order) of the things that an assistant principal may be responsible for completing while also putting a foot inside the instructional door.

The Instructional Role

How Important is It?

We know that instructional leadership is a major buzz word in the field of education. In fact, it has been for quite some time, but to varying degrees. Even before the implementation of the *No Child Left Behind Act* (NCLB) of 2001, some states were setting their own requirements, followed by assessments for accrediting schools. Instructional leadership moved to the forefront of public education with instructional accountability falling squarely on the shoulders of school principals. Some were thinking well ahead of their time or else had an inside scoop or idea as to what the federal government was thinking and thus knew NCLB (or something similar) was soon to come. Furthermore, high-stakes testing associated with accreditation standards have an impact on student graduation and thus school graduation rates, adding more pressure on school administrators.

Try telling parents that their child has passed all of his or her classes and all of the state end-of-course tests except for one (e.g., English) and consequently will not graduate with his or her peers—not an easy thing to do. With this in mind, there is no doubt that instructional leadership is in the front of the educational minds of school leaders. Strong instructional leadership is needed in such a stringent age of accountability and for the political ramifications that come with not meeting the mark. Ultimately, it is the principal who will face the political implications associated with these issues, more so than the teachers. The assistant principal is now moving into the accountability arena as a part of the administrative team via instructional responsibilities. The principal cannot do it alone; it is much too large a beast to conquer as an individual, especially as we move into higher NCLB benchmarks each year. The assistant principal has to fill in the gaps to support instruction and student achievement. On a chilly winter's day, January 20, 1961, President John F. Kennedy made the renowned statement, "Ask not what your country can do for you, ask what you can do for your country," during his inaugural address (The History Place, 2008). I would encourage assistant principals to ask what they can do for their school and for their principal.

A Need for Change

How important is instructional leadership? Well, that is a very interesting question because we have a general idea as to the answer. It is extremely important, but without always understanding what exactly instructional leadership is or maybe is not. Does having a good school make a person a good instructional leader? Does having a poorly performing school make one a bad instructional leader? We may know or have heard the saying that if we keep on doing what we have always been doing, then we will keep on getting what we have always gotten. This can sometimes present a dilemma for some school leaders because they may have a good school and may not want to jeopardize current and past successes. Then, again, if a school is performing poorly, there may be a greater need for change. Because the good school is less obvious, I spend time discussing it and the need to improve.

Why is a there need for change despite the status of the school? Good schools need to change just as poorly performing schools do, and great schools have to make changes to maintain greatness. No one can sit still because time certainly does not. But, it must be understood that by *change* I mean improvement, not change without a specific set of goals that aim to improve teaching and learning for all students. *Webster* (1983) defines change as giving a different position, course, or direction in order to undergo transformation, transition, or substitution. There is nothing negative about the definition of change, but the word seems to have a conflicted meaning in many minds. Often times change can be improperly translated into something negative as people are asked to leave their comfort zones, not realizing the potential benefits of change. Change presents opportunity and opportunity presents a chance at a better life and a better way of doing things. Steven R. Covey (2004), in *The 8th Habit:*

From Effectiveness to Greatness, shares an analogy for explaining
the difficulty of change:

> Imagine for a moment that you take a step back in time
> and are a hunter and a gatherer of food. Each day you
> go out with a bow and an arrow or stones and sticks
> to gather food for your family. That's all you've ever
> known, seen, and done to survive. Now imagine some-
> one comes up to you and tries to persuade you to be-
> come what he calls a "farmer." What do you think your
> response would be? (pp. 12–13)

Covey goes on to explain that with some hard work a great harvest is produced—a harvest 50 times greater than from hunt-
ing and gathering. He then moves on to the transformation of
farming into the industrial age and thus another 50% increase
in production occurs and finally the transition into the knowledge age with further production increases. Certainly change
was a stressor for the hunters and the gatherers, the farmers,
and the industrial age workers who seemed to be surviving
comfortably or at least surviving. The benefit was too great not
to change, not to take a risk, at least for some who were willing
to try a new idea. Where would we be today if some people
were not willing to be leaders and to create a change for a better
life? Would we still be hunters and gatherers in the twenty-first
century? It was getting people to envision what could be as opposed to what is that made a difference for the hunter and gatherers. Without vision, people are not motivated or inclined to
leave their comfort zones because they do not have any idea as
to what could be, they cannot see. Leaders have to be the eyes.

Changing Good Schools

Survival is a basic human instinct and as long as people
are surviving as they are, the idea of change will always be a
stressor because it threatens that very survival. Having basic
needs fulfilled creates a comfort zone. Many learned about basic needs when studying Maslow's hierarchy of needs (Maslow,
2002–2007). Good leaders realize this and try to instill a vision

that guides people out of their comfort zones for something better and stronger—to Maslow's highest level—self-actualization, full potential. This should be done in education as well. An unknown author (MotivateUs.com, 2008) said, "Managers fight fires, leaders light fires." Indeed, fires need to be lit to spread the kind of motivation and encouragement that makes visions realities by pulling people out of their comfort zones to self-actualization.

Certainly it is hard to argue that a school that is doing well should change its instructional practices and instructional leadership. But, I would point out that even in good schools, we are leaving children behind and not tapping into the true potential within all students. This is more noticeable as the NCLB benchmarks get higher with time. This is not to sound cliché, but to point out that this could be one's own child left behind or not guided to his or her full potential. Those who do not have children should think of it as a relative or loved one. Often, these children and their parents, who are left behind, have no voice or a voice so faint that it cannot be heard and thus there can be little pressure on schools to change, to improve, by those most in need. Good schools have an unpremeditated habit of breeding success among the status quo, whereas lower-functioning students continuously struggle for any chance of success. These schools may be considered as good or even great by 90% or more of the community, but 10% of the parents and students may label the school as poorly performing because of their child's lack of success and frustration.

This is not to say that changes in instructional leadership and practices will get every single child through school successfully, although, that is the idea. What I am advising is to consider the data and what it may reveal as educators dig deeper into it. Are there any improvements in certain populations of our school based on unchanged or current instructional practices? I feel safe that the answer is no, give or take a percentage point here and there. I would venture a guess that there would be a near-flat line if one were to graph progress. The reason may lie in the fact that although the students have changed over the years, the instructional practices have not. They have not kept pace.

The slow change in instructional practices is not a criticism of teachers as many teach in the way they were taught as students or how they were taught to teach in preparation programs. Furthermore, the approach may have generated good or favorable results in the past with the expectation that it will continue to do so in the future. Some teachers have tried or are trying to differentiate or to change their instruction, whereas others need a little more coaxing as comfort levels are tested and confidence is built. Generally, it is not that teachers do not want to change to help students, but that their comfort levels hinder it. As leaders we must instill eagerness—not anxiousness—in our teachers to make the needed changes that are known to promote student success.

Quality Leadership at all Levels

If improvements in identified struggling populations are not seen with past pedagogical practices, then an imminent change is necessary. This change must be based on data and research as to what works best for students—all students. This data and research may be unique to the school or it may be on a larger scale. Sitting down in collaborative groups and looking at the cold hard facts can be a tough and emotional thing to do, especially when viewing individual teacher data. But these collaborative groups have to look at all data (e.g., state assessments, district assessments, common teacher assessments, informal assessments, SAT scores, ACT scores, AP scores, teacher D and F reports, percent of graduates, and enrollment figures) and for all groups represented in the school to make data-informed decisions. Be sure to emphasize and focus on the good things seen in the data. Too narrow of a focus on the negative will prevent a school from moving forward. Remember, that while trying to lift up struggling students, educators must also stretch and challenge more successful students. We can ill afford to forget about these students in our data-informed decision making.

There is no substitute for quality instructional leadership and that simply is how important it is. For assistant principals who are often stuck in the managerial muck, instruction can be invigorating, refreshing, and stimulating. It can often expose the assistant principal to a different set of students who are often ignored because they fly below the assistant principal's radar (good grades, good behavior, and involved in extracurricular activities) and can give a reminder as to why we get up and come to work each day. We must always try to keep these overlooked students on our radar because they are the backbone of a school.

I recently started a Student Leadership Team in my school that is comprised of class officers from each grade level, representation from fine arts, athletics, academics, school clubs, and the student council. We meet on a monthly basis to discuss school life, school culture, school improvement, and academics. These are fairly heavy-duty topics for young people, but they always have excellent ideas and I value their input. It is very inspiring to meet with this group of young leaders and I always carry their ideas to our Staff Leadership Team for discussion. I have a great passion for student leadership and this is one way to fill it. Again, we have to carve out the time and give our undivided attention if we want such a group to be leaders within and outside the school. I was once called out of a Student Leadership Team meeting because of a fight and returned to a group that was steadily discussing the topic as if I had never departed.

There are good students, good teachers, and good things going on inside school house walls everyday that assistant principals do not always get to see or to hear about because of their constant exposure to problems that require attention. It can sometimes be just like watching the news—only the bad stuff makes it on the air while the good stuff does not seem to sell and thus is dust in the wind. Assistant principals really need to get inside those walls within their schools to see what is going on so that they can make connections and hence decisions about the direction of their instructional leadership and what to talk about with teachers. This is hard to do if we are not in the classrooms at least on a weekly basis, but daily presence is the ultimate goal. Student Leadership Teams can also tell about some of these things. They are very honest and tactful. My team gave me advice on how teachers could better use the ninety-minute block classes to get the most out of students. They asked for more interaction, more discussion, more group work, and understood that lecture was necessary, but preferred it in small doses.

Establishing Credibility

Often the problem assistant principals have when it comes to instructional leadership is credibility because teachers know that assistant principals may have very little time to spend in the classrooms as a result of putting out fires. With this in mind, the opinion may be that assistant principals are trying to train teachers instructionally when they do not know what is happening in the classrooms. This is a valid point and a key point in establishing credibility as an instructional leader. This is not to say that the staff doesn't respect the assistant principal, but it is to say that teachers may reason that the assistant principal's strongest qualities lie outside the classroom doors—in the area of management—because this is what they often observe. Again, this is because of where the assistant principal spends much of his or her time on most days. The goal is to change this mentality by getting into the classrooms.

To free up time during the instructional day, schedule some special education meetings after school, but not all, as parents have a say (by law) in determining convenient meeting times. Assistant principals have to process disciplinary infractions while the students are in school to give due process, which again is required by law, and they have to monitor lunch periods and hallways to prevent problems in highly populated environments. This consumes an hour to two of each day, but it is good preventive maintenance. Granted that even if everything else goes well, the assistant principal is left with minimal time for the quality examination of instruction or completion of other duties. This is not a big secret to most faculty and staff, who are somewhat aware of an assistant principal's day, at least on the surface. Staff may not know all the details of the job, but they do know the time restrictions. Therefore, establishing credibility in the instructional area requires a lot of creativity to free up time.

How does an assistant principal establish credibility as an instructional leader among the staff? There are several ways to do this and all should probably be done rather than just one or some of them. First, the staff has to know that the assistant principal is genuine and passionate about all of the training he or she leads. If the staff feels that the training is being done simply to check it off a to-do list, they will not care or even try to implement it because it is of no value. The assistant principal has to make a dedicated effort of getting into the classrooms on a daily basis to show that he or she is serious and excited about instruction. There will be times when this is not possible because of demands that require immediate attention. But, if an individual aims for being in classrooms only one or two times a week and something unexpectedly pops up, no time will be spent in classrooms. This is a chink in the credibility armor.

There are times that I have set out to visit ten classrooms, only to be pulled away after visiting just one, but I at least visited one! Plan on being in classrooms as much as possible and carry a radio so that you can be called in case of a true emergency. It is better to get into some classrooms rather than none, even if not as many as you would like. I always find that if I sit in my office trying to knockout some work, people or issues find me, and I stay just as busy, if not busier, than playing catchup after school on what I missed while I was visiting classrooms.

Credibility comes from demonstrated consistency and passion as an instructional leader. Consistency comes from following up on professional development that has been given to teachers. Following up means getting into classrooms on a daily basis to see the training implemented and looking for new areas in which staff development is needed and resources to support teachers. It also means providing support and clarification for teachers and that there are no repercussions for taking educationally appropriate risks to change. Let's face it, some days new things just flop. Teachers who learn from this and improve will make it work the next time and should be praised for their efforts.

Be sure to share and discuss best practices, offer praise, and follow up with notes of encouragement. Teachers cannot function in an environment that offers no praise for success and instills fear for taking chances to improve instruction. They have to feel that administrators have confidence in their abilities to best teach children. The relationship has to be one centered around a passion for instruction. As Carol Ann Tomlinson (2003) wrote, "[u]ncertainty is inherent in teaching. Although we can seldom guarantee the results of our decisions, we must make decisions, nonetheless" (p. 10). Educators must make educationally sound decisions and set forth with them to meet the needs of diverse learners and everchanging students while realizing that all will not succeed, but the effort will be made as if all will. Be mindful that I am not speaking of reckless risks, but of risks that are thought through from a pedagogical perspective as something new or different that may improve student engagement and student understanding.

Follow Up on What is Seen

Failure to visit classrooms often means some teachers may play the gambling game. That the administrator probably will not make it into their classroom and thus they can teach the way they have always taught, within their comfort zone. When administrators do make it to the classroom for a periodic visit, some teachers could produce a good lesson or two to meet the requirements of an annual evaluation. This is not a criticism of teachers; we have our comfort zones and do not feel we would teach as well if we deviate from this zone. It is more of a criticism of administrators and the system because without getting into the classrooms to check for implementation of new instructional strategies we are also sacrificing support, guidance, and clarification. Furthermore, the administrator can only become stronger and more comfortable instructionally with such experience. Without these methods of followup, there should be no expectation of implementation or improvement because there is no support being given. In addition to other types of observations, I like to pick a certain hallway and stop at every classroom on that hallway for at least a few minutes.

The good news is that followup can strengthen instructional practice and build credibility for the assistant principal as a leader of instruction. This credibility can enable easier and more accepted professional development of staff in the future. It is surprising how many teachers come back to share their experience when something worked very well. They are excited, and their excitement is contagious. The more opportunities that the assistant principal can take to deliver training to staff, collaborate with teams, and followup on training, the better the instructional program will be and the better the assistant principal will be as an instructional leader. Coaching techniques become very valuable at this point. I like to give one tip or suggestion at a time. Often this one tip will lead to other issues being corrected naturally—a domino effect. I try not to overload teachers or to have a laundry list of problems, which can be discouraging. Encourage peer observations, videotape lessons so that teachers can reflect on their performance (much like a coach does with a player), and invite teachers to present at faculty meetings or local and national conferences.

Do not just deliver training and forget that it ever happened! To do so is starting off on the wrong foot and regaining credibility could prove to be a futile task in a world already reluctant to change. This is especially true when there is a large time gap between the training and the followup with teachers. The absolute worst thing that can be done to teachers is to waste their time. They will be resentful of this and regaining their attention in the future could be a difficult task. Think how hard it may be when doing the next professional development training. Teacher time is very important and wasting it can put the administrator in the hot seat. I believe that the best thing an assistant principal can do is link staff development from one session to the next over a period of time so that there is a connection and a scaffolding process for teachers. When people make connections, they learn! Start with something, check on it, and build upon it. Our school is currently linking together a three-year plan for instructional goals and the professional development to support it. Everybody knows where we want to be in three years.

5

When and How
to Use Power: Do
I Have Any?

Power is a delicate thing and how it is used is very closely related to personality and to leadership style. *Webster* (1983) defines power as a possession of control, authority, or influence over others. As seen from this definition, there are many avenues for the use of power. How will an assistant principal use power? Power is something that comes with the position as school leader but if incorrectly used, it can make an assistant principal powerless. Power has to be used responsibly or it can have some negative side effects (e.g., animosity, hurt feelings, or toxic school culture). Although power comes with authority, it is closely related to personality, which cannot be changed easily. It is unusual to hear certain leaders who are known to have a certain demeanor deviate from that character or personality. A school leader who is known to be mild mannered and soft spoken would not typically yell or shout and get upset easily. It probably would create more curiosity and questions rather than accomplishing a purpose.

There may be leaders who do scream and shout and this may be normal and may often get results. However, these results will usually be out of fear and not respect, which is a strong use or misuse of power. Just picture that person shifting to a nice, soft, mellow tone. How would people respond? I might try to get away as quickly as possible. The mild-mannered and soft-spoken demeanor may be considered as a lack of power by some. It all depends on how a person looks at it. The bottom line is that leadership style is highly associated with personality. A tiger cannot change its stripes and individuals cannot change personality, but it can be modified slightly to fit a given environment or situation.

Leadership Styles

Determining a leadership style is not easy because it is strongly related to personality and, therefore, may not actually be a choice. Furthermore, the leadership style of the principal may serve as the barometer for which leadership style the assistant principal adopts. A leader cannot simply look at a book on leadership styles and choose from it as if it were a menu item at a restaurant. Reading a book on leadership styles can be helpful because it will make one cognizant of advantages and disadvantages of each style, but it is not the be all and end all of establishing a leadership style. It is simply a guide to the different leadership styles. There are many different people with whom assistant principals must interact who may have different leadership styles. Recognizing the leadership styles of others helps to make one a better leader because he or she is able to interact with a variety of people.

There are all kinds of websites to visit to answer a series of questions or take a leadership style quiz. The website will tally the information and give a leadership profile and a description of the characteristics related to that type of leadership. The one I completed (http://psychology.about.com/library/quiz/bl-leadershipquiz.htm) stated that I was predominately a participative leader. Be mindful that this profile does not lock me into one style, but it did tell me the style that I mostly use. Go to the Internet and search for *leadership style quiz or survey*. These types of quizzes are fun and only take a few minutes—so give it a shot. Just remember, it is only a reference. I did this with my Student Leadership Team by bringing laptops to a meeting and they really enjoyed it. We followed up with a great discussion. This could be a fun exercise with teachers as well. I encouraged teachers do this with their students to get an idea of leadership styles so that they can begin making connections, especially with the more challenging students.

Respect over Power

One leadership style cannot be used for every situation while performing the job. The situation or the person may mean shifting gears, if possible. This leads me back to respect. To gain respect means that people must be treated with respect. Respect does not necessarily come with the title. The people on the team who must get the job done in the classroom when the doors close each day must respect the assistant principal or the job may not get done. Keep in mind that there is a big difference between respecting someone and liking someone because personality plays a major role. People do not have to like to respect nor do they have to respect to like. It would be great to have both, but both are not required to lead. Earning respect is the more important of the two. Trying to get everybody to like us is a losing and time consuming game. No one can make everybody happy all the time.

When I first started as an assistant principal, a veteran administrator whom I have a great deal of respect for told me that if the assistant principal has to wear their power on their sleeve, they do not have any. He told me this as a piece of advice in a casual conversation, and I feel it is important to pass this great advice along to you. It was an interesting piece of advice for me at the time because I was a new assistant principal and had never really reflected on the use of power with the position. I guess I was naïve and just assumed that everything I wanted to get done would get done because I was in a position of power—I was the assistant principal!

I had always met demands placed on me by administrators when I was a teacher, liked or not, because I valued my job, my reputation, and I respected their position and their power as school leaders. On reflection, I should have known better and thought this through as it applied to my past experiences as a teacher. When I was a teacher and in a position of power with my students, did everything I asked them to get done occur? Of course not. This meant that I had to approach getting goals or tasks accomplished differently for students to master the content and not fail the class. It meant changing my approach to how I accomplished goals.

I did not think about the way I used my power as a teacher until high-stakes testing suddenly showed up at my classroom door. This quickly led me to reflect on how I did things now that my students' performance and, consequently, my job were under scrutiny. Prior to this, it was about managing the low number of Ds and Fs that students in my class were earning. This was not that hard to do because I could offer various forms of extra credit and makeups so that students were successful.

Because most of my students were doing well, I never thought about changing what I did as a teacher. After my first few years I thought I had it all figured out, but I did not. With the new changes in accountability (state testing and NCLB) I knew that I had to change to bring the indisposed on board. These would be the students who would make or break me on the state tests. Without getting these students on board, I would fail and suffer the consequences that came with that failure. Therefore, it is not any different as an assistant principal than it was for me as a teacher. It is just on a much larger scale.

The assistant principal has many duties, both managerial and instructional, that require teachers to do their part; however, getting 100% genuine and honest participation may be difficult. Getting the reluctant on board may be a real challenge. At times we may even wonder why we gave a directive to the staff and yet some did not complete it or follow the directions that were given. Is it because the assistant principal does not have power? Do they not respect the assistant principal? Do they not care about their job? Or do they presume that there really is not any consequence for failing to complete a task given by the assistant principal? Does tenure play a role in this? Regardless of the answers, there is a problem that must be quickly fixed. If not, the job could be on the line because tasks are not getting completed under the assistant principal's leadership or the insubordination could spread from the inside out—rotting the foundation. When this is discovered, it may be too late to fix, and starting over could be an arduous task.

The principal and the principal's superiors will not keep accepting the excuse of not completing a task because the teachers did not do their part, especially if the principal has to keep intervening to make sure it gets done, which takes up time. Eventually, the assistant principal may be told that he or she is in charge and if the job cannot be done, then perhaps somebody else should be given the opportunity—not good! This sounds very direct and harsh, but ultimately it is what may happen if the job is not completed. After all, it is a business, and a very important one. Just think of a coach who cannot get his players to do as expected and thus starts losing games and control of the team. I would venture a guess that this coach would not be around for long.

Now that the problem has been presented, what is the solution? I cannot give a solution that comes with a guarantee, but I can offer some practical advice based on several years of experience that I believe will help solve the assistant principal's puzzle. When all the expectations, training, and staff development are completed, the issue then becomes one of respect and relationship building. I discuss respect in the remainder of this chapter and relationship building in more detail in the next. Additionally, it is about a person's perception of power and what it means to him or her. An assistant principal does have power and quite a bit of it. Remember that the assistant principal is second in command at the building level, a position of authority with tremendous responsibility. Sometimes, when the principal is out of the building for job-related meetings or personal reasons, the assistant principal becomes first in command, albeit temporarily, but this is good experience, especially if nothing goes wrong.

Using Power Correctly

Parents believe that assistant principals have quite a bit of power and are held responsible for using it. This is quite evident when they call or email requesting a solution to a problem that they or their child has with a particular teacher, coach, or situation. Quite often they expect major consequences to be placed on the teacher or the coach and will state bluntly these expectations while demanding to know such outcomes of actions taken, even though personnel matters cannot and should not be shared. These types of situations are valuable learning opportunities and provide training for aspiring principals who one day may have to deal with such issues on a larger scale, especially if they escalate beyond the school building.

As can be seen and will be soon learned, there is power in the position, just like there is power in an automobile. The assistant principal just has to know how to use it, how to drive it, how to make it work for, but not against, him or her. It is improper to mash the gas pedal when maneuvering around a sharp curve on a winding road. Similarly, it is unwise to use power in the professional setting of education if it is not needed or will make a situation worse. Remember that whatever decision is made, there are always short- and long-term consequences and maybe even some undermining behavior that will occur as a result of the action taken. Dealing with human behavior is not like turning a light switch on and off. There are emotions involved, which complicate the situation, so we really need a dimmer switch to control power in a particular situation.

It is not to say that we cannot be firm, but we do have to be tactful in delivery and also remove emotions from the situation. Once this is done, respect will begin to emerge, but there is still more to it. It is important for assistant principals to observe and to learn the power structure that already exists in the building and its parameters. Taking time to do this is a wise choice and saves time in the long run. We live in a respect generation (even among adults) and must be mindful of this expectation (deserved or not). Remember that in most states it is very hard to release a tenured teacher so it is much more productive to aim for improvement than dismissal. Teachers who feel upset may try to undermine the assistant principal, but not necessarily to a point that calls for removal, but enough to make life miserable. Therefore, it is much better to get things accomplished, if possible, through relationships and respect than through power alone.

Teaching, Not Telling

I have found, just as most probably have, that telling a person to do something without an explanation is futile because there is no motivation for accomplishment. This is true with adults and with children. While there are times that an explanation is neither warranted nor required, there are many other times when an explanation, rather liked or not, will get the mission accomplished without costing the administrator anything. Remember, that ultimately, it is about getting the mission accomplished, but the process is just as important as the product when dealing with people. People may give one or two successful products because they were told to, but that is chiefly because they are dealing with the boss. Sooner or later, the because-I-said-so well will run dry, and we will now have to dig deeper, using more energy and time, and now it does cost something.

Save the use of power and firmness for when all other methods have been exhausted. At this point the assistant principal is well within his or her rights to lay down the law, respectfully, but firmly to a staff member who is blatantly insubordinate. This approach gives the assistant principal a leg to stand on when the employee now views him or her as being unfair because requests have now turned into demands along with reprimands, a fair use of power. Explain to the employee that this is no longer a matter for discussion. Numerous opportunities to address the issue have been given regarding how he or she initially wanted to handle it. To this point there was no micromanagement. But now, the ball is out of his or her court and the goal is to accomplish the task how and when it is to be completed. This may create a little tension at first, but a staff member who reflects on the situation will realize that he or she was given ample opportunity to handle the issue well before the person with power ever became involved. Had the steps of explaining the purpose been omitted and the assistant principal directly mandated that the job get done and how, the staff member might have a legitimate grievance.

Working collaboratively with people will pay long-term dividends for when issues arise in the future because the people will know that the assistant principal is not just telling them what to do, but explaining why it needs to be done and perhaps how, even if it is not a popular decision. Remember that short-term investments can have long-term benefits and are well worth it. It is wise practice to keep investing and reinvesting in people to accomplish the school's mission. Sometimes we get busy and frustrated and forget to do the upfront investment in people, paying for it down the road.

Modeling Great Leaders

The best way to use power properly and to lead people is to reflect back on certain admired people and then internalize their leadership skills. This does not have to be a school administrator, but it could be. It may be a teacher, a person from church, a person from the community, a coach, a family member, a mentor, or a well-known leader researched in the past. Think about why people really admired, respected, and adored this person. The answer to leadership lies within the responses to the following questions. Why was this particular person a great leader? What are his or her qualities? What are his or her key characteristics? And most importantly, why do I want to be like this person when leading others? The good news is that it does not have to be just one person. Leadership style could be a collage of several admired people or it could be that different characteristics of these people are applied to unique situations.

I have had the luxury to work under five different principals in three different high schools. I have kept mental and written notes through the years about the characteristics that I admired about each one. Some may be on the "do not" list as well, but I have been fortunate in my tenure as an assistant principal to work with skillful leaders. These notes include how they dealt with people, managed the building, led instruction, motivated staff, dealt with difficult situations, and earned respect from others. Each had his or her own personality and different ways of achieving goals and the school's mission. I have tried to incorporate each of their strengths into my own leadership style or to particularly difficult situations. But, it is not as simple as that. Just because there is a style or trait that is admired, does not mean that it can be emulated. Indeed, those leaders have had years of practice and experience in developing useful leadership skills and in a variety of positions.

The skills chosen to emulate must resemble an individual's personality or they must fit into the particular school culture. If they do not, it will be hard for people to take the person seriously. It just will not work. Sincerity is the best practice. Look for the comfortable traits and work on building the others that are needed as determined. Just be sure that these are attainable traits. Some may not be achieved this early in a career. Some cannot be duplicated because of personality. However, some characteristics can be duplicated, such as demeanor and compassion. The key is to be patient. Developing credibility takes time. Credibility is developed by being consistent, genuine, passionate, and modeling desired behavior.

In *The 8th Habit* (2004), Stephen R. Covey makes a wonderful analogy of leadership traits to that of the inimitable role of being a grandparent. Covey summed it up perfectly as follows:

> The most essential role of grandparents is to communicate, in as many ways as possible, the worth and potential of their children, grandchildren and great grandchildren clearly that they really believe it and act on that belief. If this spirit suffused our culture and society, the impact on the civilization of the world would be unimaginably magnificent and endless. (p. 99)

A beginning administrator will have to go through many trial and error phases before he or she truly finds a comfort zone and determines what works best to lead people to greatness, to their worth and potential. Just be aware that comfort zones can change from year to year, from teacher to teacher, and from administrator to administrator. This is quite obvious in schools with multiple assistant principals who demonstrate different leadership styles and personalities. All can be effective administrators, but it is quickly noticed that each has distinct characteristics for achieving success. Both manage to accomplish the mission of the school, but in different ways.

Modeling Expectations

With so many different students in a building and so few administrators, it is a positive for students and staff to have different personalities among administrators. I just caution assistant principals to be consistent in their actions and their consequences as students will compare notes and make judgments. Collaboration and teamwork have to be modeled and this is a good place to start. The administrative team has to collaborate and send a strong message that they are a united team that can neither be divided nor conquered in spite of having different personalities (much like a two-parent household). Although personalities may vary, the consequences for student misbehavior should not. Inconsistencies in this area can create perception of favoritism or unfairness.

Think back about the person who will be modeled as a leader. What was his or her way of motivating others? As I think back regarding my own situation, I realize that the person I admired was motivating me by giving me an opportunity and a chance to do the task better than it had ever been done before. This person tried to stretch me as a learner and as a person, which required me to step outside of my comfort zone just a little bit at a time so that failure was not an option. Consequently, this made me feel good about myself. I wanted to impress the person. I wanted to do a great job to show the person I was worthy of the opportunity given to me. In reflection, I saw that the leaders I wanted to emulate did not just give me an assignment, but an attainable challenge which would result in personal growth. Although I was not always thrilled about the challenge, I can now see the intent. The person knew that letting me do it was better than telling me the answer or how I should do it. I would venture a guess that nobody would mention a person who used negative reinforcement as a great leader, maybe a dictator, but not a leader. So do not take this approach to get things accomplished. It does not lead people to their full potential nor does it produce quality workmanship.

When people are faced with challenges and given the proper support to master such challenges, they tend to do their best work. The assistant principal must be willing to challenge people to do great things (rather than just telling and getting only mediocre results) and provide the support needed for success. This is the key ingredient in building a better and a stronger school. Leave it out and the recipe does not come to fruition. Ultimately, teachers will shut their classroom doors with their students in the classroom and conduct poor, mediocre, or great teaching of students. How a person motivates and challenges teachers to reach their full potential as an instructional leader will make all the difference as to what happens when the doors close. Do not assume that the expectations are being met, know that they are. Continually look at the data while collaborating with teachers in order to stay on the right path. Positive reinforcement and recognition are needed to build a better and a stronger school and to motivate people.

Breaking the Walls of Isolation

As a leader, just think about the quality of instruction desired for your own child (if not a parent, for a relative) and motivate and lead teachers to that level of instruction. Teachers will do a good job in the classroom if they understand why they are being asked to improve their instructional practices. Telling them to change with no explanation may result in quite a different reaction, especially if they are already doing well. This is a natural reaction and must be taken into consideration when addressing teachers. After all, the goal is to motivate, not to frustrate or underappreciate.

The most important step in improving instruction goes back to an earlier discussion in this book, which is administrative follow up for support in the classroom. This does not mean that teachers will not do what is expected because they are not being observed, but it does mean that followup for support, clarification, and encouragement are very important for making sure that all are on the same page and that successes do not go unnoticed—breaking the walls of isolation. Often times a teacher's work gets overlooked because of isolation from other teachers and administrators. This makes it difficult for positive reinforcement because it cannot be recognized if no one knows about it. In *Results Now*, Mike Schmoker (2006) quotes J. I. Goodland as saying, "Isolation ensures that new learning seldom leads to changes in practice—in what teachers teach or how well they teach" (p. 26). Additionally, Schmoker points to Harvard's Tony Wagner as writing of how enforced isolation ensures that "[m]ost of us in education are mediocre at what we do" (p. 27).

Isolation is another adversary of greatness. Teachers often do not get a chance to see what other teachers are doing in their classrooms. Sometimes it must be brought to them because logistics simply prevent it. Getting into classrooms to see the good things that are happening and then sharing them with the staff at faculty meetings and professional development sessions can be very inspiring to teachers. This is the fun stuff for assistant principals. Do not let the good things go unnoticed and unrecognized. These good things are not known if they are not seen. Consequently, groundbreaking ideas are not spread from one teacher to the other. Again, power could be used to accomplish or try to accomplish instructional goals, but the level of quality would be much lower and the time spent in classrooms would be more about checking things off a list of expectations as opposed to having a good time interacting with teachers and students.

Supporting Teachers While Breaking Comfort Zones

Teachers (or anybody else for that matter) tend not to perform well if they feel their job is hanging over their head based on their perception of administrators regarding evaluations. I would much rather go into a classroom to see new strategies in action and interact with the students than to simply be checking for rote duplication of expectations from a standard formative observation form. This can be stressful to teachers. Remember that there are several ways that teachers have of meeting evaluation requirements. Allow them to be creative enough to choose the ones that best benefit children based on their expertise and which they are most comfortable attempting. They should not worry about getting marked down for classroom management because they have an activity that requires movement around the classroom which may generate a little noise. I would much rather see this than students who are passively engaged and dead quiet. Teachers need to know this up front or they will be afraid to take risks. In an *Educational Leadership* article about how compliance influences classroom practice, Allison Zumda (2008), posed a powerful question: "To what extent do the classroom rules encourage the "neatness" of compliant behavior instead of compliant behavior instead of the inherent messiness of engagement?" (p. 41). Sometimes, teachers sacrifice what is best for students for the compliance they think administrators want to see. Somewhere in a classroom hangs a poster that reads, "You may never make a discovery if you are afraid to make a mistake." Administrators should support teachers in their quest for discovery.

Building confidence a little at a time is the key for breaking comfort-zone barriers. It can be analogized to a child starting off with training wheels on a bike and then eventually removing those wheels. There may be some bumps, and wobbling at first, but steadiness and mastery eventually evolve with each successful ride. Power should be put in the bank and used for a time when it is truly needed. Motivation and encouragement will get more out of people and allow them to do new and creative things to benefit children because they are not afraid of failure and consequences for trying. Additionally, people will be motivated to produce the best product possible as they work in an environment that supports appropriate risk taking and recognizes successes. As these teachers share their successes, new learning leads to changes in practices for others, and the walls of isolation begin to crumble.

6

Relationship Building: Cannot Get Far Without It

This chapter ties in well with some of the information I shared in the previous chapter on power. As a refresher, that chapter dealt with the use of motivation and encouragement as a substitute for power, using power only when necessary. This chapter expands upon that and discusses how such leadership, motivation, and encouragement will result in positive relationship building. An assistant principal needs to build relationships with a variety of stakeholders. These include, but are not limited to, teachers, support staff, students, parents, community members, central office personnel, and school board personnel.

Investing time in relationship building with stakeholders is crucial in achieving success as an assistant principal. This is especially true during those times when it is necessary to make unpopular decisions as they cross the desk or are pushed down from a higher power. Because time has been taken to build a genuine relationship with the person or group, that person or group is more willing to give the benefit of the doubt, allowing the assistant principal to maintain credibility as a leader and as a relationship builder while accomplishing the unpopular task. This is not to say that making unpopular decisions all of the time is a good idea because that will eventually be perceived as a misuse of power or having a lack of sincerity. However, if people have trust, the chances of accomplishing detested tasks are better. Trust takes time to develop. Sometimes it can take three or more years. Again, just be patient and work on it day to day.

Ultimately, there are going to be times when it is necessary to make a decision that is out of one's control and these will be the times that relationships are put to the test. However, if there has been no relationship built in the past, it is not possible to get people on board when making unpopular decisions or enacting change in the future. This is not a good situation to be in at all, never. There have been many times in my career as an assistant principal that I have had to sit down as part of an administrative team to make decisions that we knew would result in the staff being unhappy and we dreaded the delivery of the information and subsequent reaction. This is a natural and expected part of the job. Often these decisions are more about shooting the messenger than the culprit, but a leader has to take it on the chin to show that the school can survive such an unpopular mandate.

Blaming unpopular decisions on others such as the central office and acting like the decision is not supported by passing the proverbial buck is poor leadership, and in due course will make the person look bad as the task will not get accomplished without support and leadership. There is no easy way out of problems that do not have obvious answers or any answer at all. Thus relationship building is the key to being a successful leader. A leader who is trusted and respected because of the time taken to build relationships will be successful in any storm because the stakeholders will stick with him or her during the good and the bad times, serving as the foundation. This does not mean it will be easy or without emotion, but the support will be there.

Relationship Building and Earning Trust

Relationship building is more than just having people stay when the bad times come knocking on the door. It is also about trust and with trust among staff members comes many opportunities to build a better and a stronger school from which students will ultimately benefit. Furthermore, trust allows for the free flow of information sharing, which is important in completing tasks related to the assistant principalship. Relationship building is not restricted to just the adults in the building. People of all ages have to learn and exercise relationship-building skills. Students with whom a relationship has been built are more likely to come in trust with confidential information that is paramount to school safety and security. This may be information about something that has happened, that is being investigated or something big being planned for the future that may result in vandalism, injury, or even death. If the administrators do not develop these types of relationships with students, gathering such information will be nearly impossible and very time-consuming. Teachers who have built relationships with students are also a barometer for what is going on in and out of the building.

As a new assistant principal or new to a particular building, it is important to realize that relationship building and trust will take some time. Be patient and do not force it. This will delay the ability to develop trust. It may take several months to a full school year or several years. As the assistant principal is watching the students, they are watching the assistant principal, and there are many more eyes than one may think. Every move is being evaluated and credibility is being determined regardless of reality or perception.

People will remember and judge the assistant principal for what has been done, what has been said, and what is going to be done. Do not make threats or promises that are not carried through, especially not on a consistent basis. The people being led talk with one another. This is what I refer to as parking lot talk. Perceptions are quickly formed this way without people having all of the facts. This is typical human nature and must be accounted for as a leader.

Always Being Watched

An assistant principal has to watch over an entire team. The staff is only watching the assistant principal and maybe one or two other administrators, depending on how supervision is divided and the number of administrators. Therefore, the actions that people see are very important because they have to decide if what the administrators are saying coincides with what their eyes are seeing. If I assign several teachers to lunch supervision duty and inform them of the expectations I have, such as being on time, standing and moving around the cafeteria, and cleaning up after the students leave, but I do not model these behaviors, I will be labeled as lazy or too good to do the work I expect of teachers. If other assistant principals do a good job at this and I do not, I will get a bad reputation among teachers.

This word does not take long to get around the building. This makes change very difficult. On the other hand, modeling the expectations and collaborating with the other teachers on lunch duty will create a reputation as a hard worker and a leader who is willing to do the same work expected of the entire staff. This word will spread as well and will do wonders to build relationships with staff members.

People like to be led by those who are team players and by those who do not view themselves as better than the team. Do not be afraid to roll up the sleeves and get dirty. Dress professionally for the job, but understand it is possible to get a little dirty. Leaders need to be able to walk beside those they lead and not always in front of them. I really enjoy seeing the people I lead step up and take initiative no matter how complex or simple the task. This tells me that they are capable of dealing with certain issues should I not be there at the time. Creating leaders at all levels is how all schools become better and stronger.

Providing Recognition

Part of relationship building is providing recognition to those who are deserving of it. This can be as simple as an email or a note. People who work very hard simply because it is the right thing to do and because it is in the best interest of students should be recognized for their passion and their commitment. It does not matter if it is part of the job or not. Great accomplishments should be acknowledged. We know, or have an idea, about what the research says about internal and external motivators. Sure a bigger paycheck is a great thing, but a short-lived motivator because it is extrinsic (an outside motivator). When the money is spent, we still have to get down to the business of educating children in such a complex society. This requires internal motivation, which leaders have to inspire among those who are being led.

People who put in long hours and do great things on their own initiative will soon see their work as futile if their efforts are not noticed or recognized. Good things that happen in the classroom tend to stay in the classroom because of isolation, unless somebody notices and opens the doors to let the good things spread to other classrooms. The administrator has to be the key to opening the good classroom doors. We just have to know which doors to open, which can only be known by being in the classrooms. Although some people may work by going above and beyond the job description, they will not do it for long if they do not feel appreciated, which I understand. There are simply too many variables competing for their time. Notice I did not say anything about being paid, but recognized and appreciated for their time. The administrator has to be mindful of this and cognizant of the happenings in the building. This is especially true when it comes to innovative instructional practices in the classrooms. Depending on geographic location, the assistant principal may also have to work within permissible guidelines of the collective bargaining unit to consider the extra time that teachers put in to accomplish their goals.

As creatures of habit we tend to work within our comfort zone and when we deviate from our comfort zone we feel a loss of control and thus a loss of purpose in our lives. Consequently, changing ingrained instructional practices can be a large and scary step for teachers and for administrators. It must be done in small increments so as to build confidence and momentum and without fear of repercussions for failure. When teachers succeed at trying new instructional practices, it must be noticed, acknowledged, and shared by administrators (e.g., faculty meetings, faculty newsletter, and professional development). It does not matter how big or how small of a success it is. This is what Mike Schmoker (2006) refers to as "celebrating small successes." This is noteworthy because there is really no such thing as getting to the end when it comes to changing instructional practices. It is a journey with no end and because it is a long journey, it requires frequent recognition and celebration along the way to maintain motivation and passion. Pedagogical practices have no definite end because they are ever evolving and changing with the students who come through the schoolhouse doors and because of the changing federal, state, and local mandates.

Coaching for a Championship

Educators are endlessly researching and trying new methods of getting information into the minds of all the children and for this very reason recognition should be given, where deserved. It would be very easy in many cases for teachers to continue with past practices and still obtain acceptable or even high pass rates, but we know that unless it is a 100% rate, someone's child is being left behind. Furthermore, these pass rates do not begin to tell educators if the minds of more-prepared students are being stretched to promote growth. Could these students be doing better? Now that years of data have shown the profile of students who are passing high stakes tests, it is time to look more closely at those who are not. Better yet, it is time to look not only at data, but also it is time to look at instructional practices associated with data. It would be hard to argue that the two are not closely related.

Because assistant principals cannot be in all classrooms everyday, they must rely on relationship building and trust to carry the torch when they cannot be in the classroom. This relationship building ensures that the assistant principal and the teacher have discussed collaboratively what is best for student engagement and student learning. All of this is based on formal and informal data, which the teacher should be able to easily and freely access. It is not about scolding the teacher; it is about brainstorming and bouncing ideas off each other as professional educators. It is coaching for a championship or preparing for the big event. It is about the teacher feeling that he or she has a voice in instructional methodology and that expertise from within is part of the final decision-making process. After all, teachers are the ones who have to step into the classroom to perform, much as the athlete has to step onto the field or the actor on the stage. Just as an athlete will tell the coach what is happening on the field so that adjustments can be made, a teacher should be able to do the same as it relates to the data and to the classroom.

Dealing with Staff Stressors

Relationship building is a way of communicating with staff regardless of their status, position or job. After all, everybody in the building has the same mission, which is educating as best as possible the children who walk through the school doors. The mission has to be reflected in the daily actions of all leaders in the building. This educating may be direct (formal) or indirect (informal), but still holds the same core values. We all, for a variety of reasons, know the importance of a quality education. A parent can definitely relate to wanting educators to have the child's best interest at heart. However, teaching children can be an extremely difficult, challenging, and frustrating job that demands much patience. It is a bittersweet profession. Sometimes, educators find themselves spending more time with other people's children than with their own, and oftentimes, with no appreciation. The daily grind can lead to burnout and, subsequently, less effort in the classroom than what normally would be found because of mental or physical exhaustion or both. Relationship building with teachers can help ease this tension. It can determine when and where additional help or resources are needed or it can provide an avenue for a teacher to vent or to ask for suggestions or for help.

Teachers who believe they can talk with their administrators and walk away from the conversation feeling supported and better are much more likely to be productive in the classroom. These conversations can be formal or informal. As an administrator it is refreshing to be able to sit down and talk with teachers at the lunch table or talk with teachers in the main office or hallways about things that have nothing to do with the job. This is an opportunity for everybody to realize that there is life outside the schoolhouse walls. Education is such an isolating profession that a desire for the opportunity to see and to communicate with each other is both natural and necessary. Just reflect on how hard it is to get faculty meetings started when all of these teachers are pulled together in the same room who have not seen or talked to each other in weeks. Not an easy thing to do. Establishing relationships with staff goes well beyond casual conversations. As an administrator, good times and bad times occur in no particular order and with no particular reason.

Leading the School Family During Emotional Times

The people putting it on the line each and every day also have lives outside school. There is sorrow and happiness in their lives and a leader has to be sensitive and attentive to both as they can impact job performance. Attending funerals is probably the most difficult of all, but it is necessary to provide support in a time of grieving. Sadly, through my administrative years, I have witnessed the deaths of parents, relatives, spouses, my own staff, and saddest of all—teachers' own children and our own students. Not attending funerals or visitations or acknowledging sympathy in some way (card, flowers, food, and visitations) can be portrayed as being insensitive and only concerned about the person as an employee and not as a human being, which is not the nature or the intent of education.

When it comes to the death of a student, all eyes are on the administration, and how they handle the loss as a leader. This is very difficult and requires bringing the staff together as one to help all who are in mourning. Staff and students will have to lean on each other in these difficult times and administrators have to be sensitive to this. The loss of a student can be very devastating to many people and for a long period of time. It is important to keep an eye on everybody for several months or longer to know how they are adapting to the loss.

Funerals are one of the things in life that may actually get harder with time because they weigh so heavy on the heart and on the soul. Sometimes there is nothing to say to loved ones, but a hug will do just fine. On a more positive note, there are celebrations, such as births, weddings, and individual accomplishments of staff members or their children. Again, it is important to recognize these joys in life and to spread the word to others. These are proud moments and should be shared accordingly. Remember this is needed in such an isolating profession. As was the case with the former, it is equally important to be more than just the boss at work. As an administrative team, it is important to figure out how to best handle these details because dealing with emotions is an important part of leadership and doing nothing is detrimental.

Balancing Relationships with the Mission

Often, people in a position of power or authority are so concerned about crossing the professional line of a working relationship with an assumed inappropriate personal relationship that they fail at doing the right thing. I am not referring to inappropriate intimate relationships, but general friendships. This can stunt growth in a school community and counteract all attempts to build a better and a stronger school. It is my sincere belief that we are professionals and someone taking advantage of a superior because there is a relationship is very rare and easily correctable should it occur. Administrators need to use balance in relationship building and to adjust this balance per each situation. In the field of education we strive to model the behavior that we expect from our students, especially as future citizens for which our livelihood will one day depend. Modeling relationships and showing that we are united is a good lesson for students to observe because they are watching everything we do.

Remember that relationship building is not just between the assistant principal and the teachers. Forging relationships includes secretaries, custodians, cafeteria staff, students, parents, and community members. I was once told by a professor just before I began student teaching that the secretary, custodian, and cafeteria manager are the most important people in the building and that I should seek these people out first and introduce myself. I have found this to be quite true. Anybody who has spent time in the field of education quickly learns that a school does not function well without a team of dedicated people working cohesively. Trying to accomplish the mission of the school as a group of individuals working independently is unproductive. In *Results Now*, Mike Schmoker (2006) cited a quote by Robert Eaker that encapsulates what should be avoided in schools: "The traditional school often functions as a collection of independent contractors united by a common parking lot" (p. 23). Certainly, we do not want our one thing in common, our reputation as a school, to be that we park our vehicles in the same lot and thus this becomes our place of unification, our focal point.

Students quickly figure out who is on board as a team member and who is not. They know when people are working together and when they are not. Students are smart and intuitive when it comes to what they can get away with and what they cannot. Educators have to be very careful about this. Forgetting that educators are always under the microscope can lead to problems down the road. A classic example is when students are permitted to listen to music devices and wear hats in one class, but not in another because that teacher is following the school policy. This type of inconsistency can create rifts between teachers and confusion among students. Healthy and professional relationships must exist among teachers. Teachers have to be able to work together and show respect for one another so that students do not give teachers unjustified labels just because some are following school rules or holding high academic expectations for students. They all have to be on the same team, even if it means sacrificing popularity.

Respect at All Levels

Although teachers should be able to maintain their autonomy, creativity, and student rapport in the classroom, they should understand that we are in the profession of educating young people for the future, which should not be sacrificed for being well-liked or popular by side-stepping the rules. Teachers have to respect each other both directly and indirectly because students are always watching and comparing notes on teacher differences. As a result, students develop opinions that may or may not have merit, but can still stigmatize a teacher regardless. These inequities must be addressed immediately with teachers because they are toxic to the school culture. In such cases, I have found that clearly stated and written expectations with documented followup works best. Some things just are not flexible. This is one of them. Be sure to address these issues immediately and firmly with teachers who are not in compliance.

Everybody is watching how people are treated by the assistant principal. How are teachers, secretaries, bus drivers, custodians, and cafeteria workers treated? Are they all treated as equals? Do their suggestions or ideas carry any weight or merit? If the answer is no, the chances are that relationship building is missing and thus school goals are not being accomplished, unless through fear or micromanagement, which brings us back full circle to the issue of power. How can others be expected to perform a desired behavior if we are not modeling it ourselves? However, if the answer to treating people equally is yes, then the administrator is well on his or her way to building positive and productive relationships with the people needed for the school to succeed.

Most people would quickly answer yes to the questions posed above, for which I am pleased. However, reflect back on the questions to see if the answer is yes all of the time and in all situations. We often get very busy and sometimes sacrifice the relationship for putting out the fire. These are the times when relationship building can be put to the test and the assistant principal should always be cognizant of this slippery slope. Talking down or angrily, although unintentionally, to a colleague when stressed or busy may be a catalyst for the colleague to feel embarrassed and become resentful. This leads employees to view the administrator as hot and cold and confuses them as to when it is a good or a bad time to approach for important questions. This may lead to the employee making an impulse decision that ultimately may cost more time than having the initial discussion probably would have. The best thing to tell an employee who approaches at a bad time is that this is an extremely busy time and that he or she should come back when undivided attention can be dedicated to his or her issue or question. But realize that this approach still requires proper tone and body language to be accepted as fair.

Meeting the Needs of the Staff

We often expect the people we work with to be able to read our body language and assume that they should know we are busy, preoccupied, or moving toward a specific destination. We know what they say about assuming! The approach to meet later only has credibility if the promise is kept and the assistant principal actually meets with that person. Remember that they too are busy. Requesting to meet later and not holding up the end of the deal only results in mistrust and reservation, which is not a good ingredient in relationship building or school success. In some cases, secretaries can be empowered to relay sentiments or be able gatekeepers. This requires communication with the secretary so that there are no misunderstandings or miscommunications, which could result in additional time cleaning up a mess.

There are times when I know I just cannot keep an appointment (either initial or rescheduled) because of situations that develop during the day, so I find that employee to say I cannot meet. If it is something quick, I will meet for a few minutes if that person is still available. Seeking out colleagues and meeting them in their comfort zones can be important in relationship building. To have them constantly coming by the office to see if the door is open and then fretting over whether to knock if it is closed can be quite stressful and frustrating. Additionally, the teacher's domain can be a good place to meet because the constant interruptions that occur in the assistant principal's office are often absent in the teacher's classroom or office when students are not present.

Meeting in the teacher's domain may give one a chance to see pictures or mementos on their desks providing an opportunity to ask about family and other things on which they place value and passion. This is not to say that it is necessary to spend a great deal of time talking about it, but taking a few minutes to discuss what has been seen can be positive in fostering a relationship and showing an interest outside a professional relationship. In any case, we are all human beings with emotions, passions, and a desire to be acknowledged. Showing the people who work for us that we also have these traits will work far better than portraying that we are incapable of caring. A great idea given to me is to keep a file box with a three-inch by five-inch note card for each faculty member. Each file card is used to jot down information gleaned from informal meetings and conversations (e.g., children, hobbies, vacations, and recent trips) about the specific faculty member. We also have a Faculty Friendship Team that celebrates major events and milestones throughout the school year. This is a great way of meeting the needs of staff members.

Relationship Building is a Team Effort

It takes effort to build relationships, but the reward is ultimately beneficial to the students and to the assistant principal as a leader and as a person. I believe students who are educated in a school where there is collaboration and mutual respect among adults will graduate with a greater advantage than those exposed to a fragmented and disjointed faculty. It simply comes down to a matter of teamwork versus individuals working in isolation toward no unified goal. Anyone who has played on a team is well aware of the saying that there is no "I" in "Team." There is no "I" in faculty or staff either. There has to be genuine relationships among the whole staff for a school to be productive. There has to be leadership at all levels. Alexander Graham Bell (Learning To Give, 2008) said, "Great discoveries and improvements invariably involve the cooperation of many minds. I may be given credit for having blazed the trail but when I look at the subsequent developments I feel the credit is due to others rather than to myself" (p. 1). Bell had a vision, but he knew it would take a team of leaders to see his vision to fruition, and when it happened, the credit would need to be given to the whole team, not solely the leader or an individual.

Relationship building has to be everywhere and at all levels between all adults and students in the building. A school that has this type of climate and culture is well on its way to becoming a better and a stronger school. It is a positive place. We cannot afford to stand on the sidelines and watch the principal do all the leading and relationship building. We are in a leadership position too, and although we may want to emulate the principal's relationship skills, we can ill afford to wait to learn all of these skills. A typical school building has only one principal and one or more assistant principals. Requiring the principal to do all of the relationship building is a burden much too heavy for the principal to carry. Additionally, the kind of relationship that the assistant principal builds may be quite different from those of the principal based on the people with whom he or she interacts the most.

The position of assistant principal is one of leadership and demands that we start building relationships as soon as we begin the position. Lost time results in lost relationships. Relationship building will take some trial and error, some give and take, and plenty of collaboration with fellow administrators. Some relationships just may never happen at all, but many genuine attempts have to be made. If it benefits students, we must become great at doing it! Remember the goal is to build a better and a stronger school. It cannot be done alone, so start building relationships now and take notes on lessons learned for later.

A great way to build relationships with students is to participate in pep rallies, assemblies, and fund-raising activities. Yes, the students will usually ask us to humiliate ourselves in some way, shape, or form. But it gives them a chance to see our more human side. Remember that for some students we are their only role model and these are the students who are deciding if we are worthy of a relationship, but we have to be approachable. We have to be cool! Some of the things I have done in the past include pudding wrestling, donkey basketball, dunking booth, faculty line dances, student–faculty basketball games, pie in the face, tug-o-war, thespian skits, student job interviews, and dressing up in silly clothes. I was not always thrilled leading up to these activities as I do have some pride, but I always walked away feeling really good inside because the students applauded, chanted my name, and thanked me. It really is fun, and it is necessary to change roles and take off the assistant principal's hat. Sometimes this is hard to do because we think of activities like pep rallies as only supervisory roles and not fun or opportunistic roles, but give it a chance.

7

Collaboration with the Staff and the Principal: Preparing for the Next Level

Schools can be unique places when it comes to analyzing collaborative practices among staff members. There seems to be a combination of sorts that keeps the spread of collaboration to a minimum in schools. This ranges from the physical school design, to staff scheduling, to individual teacher comfort zones, to bell schedules, resulting in a system of isolation that continues in spite of all the research on the benefits of collaboration. These are all valid reasons as to the current state of collaboration in schools. Administrators are no exception to these reasons. Because some administrators probably spent time in isolated environments as teachers, collaboration is not an ingrained trait, but one in which experience is extremely limited, and thus comfort zones are tested. It has to be practiced over and over until it becomes a learned trait, a habit.

Although we know the importance and benefits of collaboration, we may find it difficult to find the time to expose ourselves and our staff to collaboration that has a clearly intended purpose. Too often when it does exist, it is hurried, and the gaps of time between collaboration are so great that there is no true continuity and thus no commitment from most teachers, which is understandable. It would be like a player who practices for a game only once or twice a month. It is hard to focus and to be productive when planning, grading, sponsoring extracurricular activities, and making parent contacts are weighing on one's mind along with personal commitments. These are some of the things that may prevent teachers from giving their undivided attention on staff development days, which are usually squeezed in, on, or near the end of marking periods, when grades are due, or at the beginning of the school year, when anxiety is high. I am clearly aware of this phenomenon, as I find it hard to concentrate on future plans when immediate deadlines rob my attention. Eventually, we have to prioritize our workload, and this means that those things with deadlines will get first priority. Imagine a teacher who did not get grades turned in for report cards and justified it to the principal by saying that the time was used for collaboration instead. How would the principal respond? Unfortunately, those things without deadlines or paper trails tend to suffer, regardless of their importance to student learning. This, again, creates a puzzle for administrators at all levels of public education.

Working Through the Logistics

We know the right thing to do as teachers and as administrators, but we also know that logistical circumstances constantly work against us, such as the traditional bell schedule, which dictates that all students, regardless of need, proceed through the same schedule each day. Note that I am not talking about state-mandated hours, but the inflexible daily student bell schedule that treats all students the same. I am not talking about the different scheduling models such as the traditional six or seven periods, alternating block, or four by four. I am talking about schedules that do not permit for adequate collaboration among staff members, other than on their own noncontract time. I am talking about bell schedules that only permit optional, fragmented remediation, not mandatory, systemic remediation. Fortunately, we have many educators who put in many extra hours of collaboration and preparation to improve instructional practices because they know that the students win in the long run as a result of such efforts. The problem is that all teachers do not do this, through no fault of their own, and thus the quality of a child's education can become dependent on the luck of the draw, which teacher the student ends up with when the master schedule is completed.

This is not a system that is equitable to students or to parents and often undermines parental expectations of a quality education when they send their child to school. All parents should be able to send their child to school with the expectation that no matter who their child's teacher is, the quality will be approximately the same, which should be an education with value. It is all about creating a level playing field, which we know is sometimes not the case, or mostly not the case within a single school, let alone a district, state, or country. Does collaboration among educators ensure that students have a level playing field? My answer would be that if a guarantee is being asked for, the answer is no because there are certain uncontrollable extraneous factors to consider, such as student attendance. However, if asking if it helps or if it is as close to a guarantee as possible, I would say yes. Collaboration helps to ensure that all of the educators in a building are on the same page and that all of the educators are working together like a well-oiled machine to produce a quality education for all children. Strong collaboration results in solutions to identified problems.

Collaboration: Not Just for Teachers

Collaboration involves all of the adults in the building, not just teachers. Everybody has to work hard to accomplish the mission of the school. If there are individuals not doing their part, the school may still run, but not like a well-oiled machine. Collaboration among teachers is very important, but not the know all and end all of public education. It is a large part of the desired well-oiled machine. Yes, it is vital and necessary and probably is a big piece to the instructional puzzle, but the smooth running machine needs other things, other parts to work, for proper functioning. Collaboration has to exist between teachers and administrators for the building of a stronger and a better school. Collaboration between teachers and administrators fosters relationship building and incorporates administrators in dialogue and data analysis that otherwise may not happen. It allows administrators to see past their required periodic formative observations or daily "pop ins" into a world of dialogue among teachers to improve instruction, assessment, and student achievement. Collaboration of this type really permits an administrator to roll up the sleeves and dig deeply into fresh data. Some things to look for are trends, red flags, differences among teachers on common assessment topics, strengths, weaknesses, *No Child Left Behind* (NCLB) indicators, and identified at-risk student performance.

Administrators and teachers should be comfortable with analyzing the data and should not be overwhelmed by it. Use the data that is practical and that can easily be transferred into improved instructional practices. For example, are there consistent differences between male and female test scores in a particular subject or classroom? If so, the team can now brainstorm as to why and the strategies needed to correct it. Is it about engagement, interest, or teaching methodology? Looking at the data allows administrators to see the big picture as to what is going on inside and outside the classrooms. It provides a link for brainstorming between teachers and administrators and it provides an avenue for administrators to input their advice while also listening to the advice of teachers. Do not use the data to be negative, but instead to motivate and to encourage change. Build on the positive and do not drown in the data.

Starting a Collaborative Culture

If done correctly, collaboration allows the assistant principal to put his or her thumb on the pulse of instruction while allowing the content experts, the teachers, to do their thing—teach. Remember, all the managerial duties have not suddenly disappeared, so micromanagement is not the key to student success or to instructional leadership. Fostering a collaborative environment among the experts is a good starting point. A collaborative environment may start small by meeting with only a few teachers. It may be that it starts with a book club on current best practices. Try to line up teacher duty or planning periods for collaboration or hold meetings after school. Informal collaboration can be just as important as formal collaboration. I see teachers do this all the time (e.g., brief conversations in the hallway, lunchroom, and teacher mailroom). The important thing is to start because the good things will not spread by themselves. The assistant principal should be a member of a collaborative team and not the know all, end all. If this is the case, there is no need for collaboration, just directives from the administrator. Teachers then would respond by taking on the "why bother" attitude and rightfully so, because their ideas, opinions, and expertise mean nothing if there is no room for their input.

Another important detail is that teachers who are trying to change have to understand that there are no consequences for genuine efforts to improve student achievement and no repercussions for taking risks that make pedagogical sense. As long as teachers are working as a team to improve instruction and to clearly identify what to keep and what to discard, then the administrator needs to accept and trust their expertise. If teachers are taking risks without reviewing data and making ill-informed changes or modifications, then the students suffer and are put at risk, and an intervention is both called for and necessary. However, a part of collaboration is to foster a checks and balances system so that what works stays and what does not work goes to the dumpster. It is about improving what works to make it better and to make it better for all teachers instructing that subject and all students taking that subject.

Creating a Level Playing Field for Students

It is interesting, but not surprising to find that if several teachers are instructing the same subject, they all have a set of strengths and weaknesses. It is very difficult for a teacher in this country to be an expert in all aspects of a subject because of our system of large amounts of material being covered in a short period of time. Additionally, every teacher has different interests or favorites within their subject, just as students do. The key is matching up teachers so that they can help each other where strengths and weaknesses may exist within their content areas. This is easier said than done because we really do not know other than from anecdotal evidence as to what those strengths and weaknesses may be, but the teachers know. They may not share this until they develop trust with colleagues via collaboration. Also, data can illustrate such differences, but the data has to come from the same source for a valid comparison. For data to be accurate in showing such differences as strengths and weaknesses, all teachers must start on a level playing field.

A level playing field refers to what teachers teach in the classroom—the curriculum. How can we get a true baseline if we are teaching different things or our own version of the curriculum? Thus it is important that teachers get together before and at other times throughout the school year to lay out a curriculum map based on an agreed upon interpretation of the curriculum guide. Teachers can then share lesson plans, develop common assessments, and determine how data will be analyzed and used. This collaboration is important for the interpretation of the curriculum guides as this interpretation can vary from teacher to teacher. Once this is accomplished, teachers can be said to be on a nearly level playing field and can use their own creativity for the delivery of the curriculum.

Student abilities will vary among the class sections just as they do in life. Typically, it would be hard to compare one class with many special education students to a class with few to none. Working with guidance for appropriate scheduling is a start for this problem of balancing numbers. If a balance cannot be created because of things like a coteaching program between the special education and general education teacher, the collaborative team should brainstorm for strategies to help the teacher with the heavy load of special education students to succeed. Perhaps coteaching is already helping with this issue.

The Power of Assessment

Collaborative teams may and probably should, depending on the number of students affected, include a special education teacher. It could be that a particular class period or section does not provide a good comparison and if some statistical math cannot be done to account for obvious differences such as in special education numbers, then the comparisons should be left to other classes that are more evenly balanced. Nonetheless, common assessment data from teacher determined curriculum and lesson plans begin to create a picture of where teachers and students are strong and where improvement is needed and this can be addressed in collaboration sessions. The common assessments have to be related to the common curriculum.

In his book *Test Better, Teach Better: The Instructional Role of Assessment* (2003), W. James Popham emphasizes the relationship between teaching and testing:

Just about everyone realizes that if a teacher does a great instructional job, that teacher's students will usually perform better on tests. It's the other side of the equation that's less often understood, namely, that *how* a teacher tests—the way a teacher designs tests and applies test data—can profoundly affect *how well* that teacher teaches. (p. 1)

Popham goes on to explain that teachers will teach better and students will learn more when there is a connection between teaching and testing. As educators, we need to collect both informal and formal data to make appropriate decisions or inferences about students' abilities. These inferences will help to guide instructional decisions thus applying the data.

Popham goes to great lengths to make us aware of the link between teaching and testing and assistant principals should be aware of this advice and have such discussions with their teachers as data is discussed. Once we have taken all of the necessary steps leading up to the test, give the test, and score the test, we have to do something positive with the data to improve future teaching, learning, and assessment. We cannot separate teaching and assessment. We cannot just return the test or paper to students and move on to the next topic without holding students and teachers accountable for learning from their mistakes. Often, tests and papers are returned and then discarded by the student with little to no reflection or accountability to correct obvious learning flaws. We should encourage teachers to self-assess and self-reflect and give them ownership of the road to their student's success. We can do this by coaching and encouraging teachers to work together when developing assessments and reviewing assessment data.

As an assistant principal it is important to sit down and look at data with teachers. It is good for teachers to get an outside perspective on what they are looking at as well as to hear ideas on how they can improve. Remember that assistant principals are in and out of many classrooms and not isolated like teachers and have seen what great teaching looks like. Assistant principals see what works and what does not. Therefore, the assistant principal should be well-versed with best practices.

Again, these collaborative sessions are not about reprimanding teachers, which should never be done in public or in a collaborative group setting, but about working together for improvement while encouraging teachers to work together as a team. As a coach, constructive criticism and encouragement are warranted and needed, but it has to be positive. The reprimanding, if needed, should only occur for deliberate indifference toward the mission of the school and only in private.

Supporting the Principal by Understanding the Vision

As an assistant principal it is extremely important to have a wide open channel of communication with the principal. It is important to build on the strengths of the principal while supporting the principal where he or she is not as strong—that is, you have to fill in the gaps. This is working as a team in which each member has a recognized set of strengths and weaknesses. The number one job is to make the principal's instructional vision a reality. Ask the principal to share his or her dissertation, publications, instructional goal-setting plans, educational or annual operating plans, and long-term goals. Ask if he or she needs help with school initiatives or if it is possible to attend meetings with the superintendent or to cover other applicable meetings. If time is not spent talking with the principal, then there will be no true idea of what that vision is or how to carry it out in the future. It takes many formal and informal conversations, observations, readings, and partnered activities to get a grasp on what the principal really sees for the school in the future.

Although a vision can be written as a statement to post around the building, a few sentences do not give it justice. It has to be reflected in the day-to-day operation of the school. It has to have action. If people do not see action, the vision will quickly vanish into thin air. Collaborating with the principal ensures that there is no misunderstanding of what is expected of the assistant principal and no ambiguity in how to meet those expectations. Additionally, collaborating with the principal will indicate what type of latitude is afforded in decision making about instructional strategies to meet the goals that the principal has set for the school. Talk about instruction early and often so that both are on the same page. A point will eventually be reached when it is possible to anticipate what the other is thinking.

Learning From the Principal

An assistant principal can learn much from the principal. I have found that every principal I have worked for, or every leader whom I model, has a tremendous set of experiences and wisdom to bring to the table. It is crucial to have an appetite for eating at this table and not be hesitant to sit at this table and converse. If one is not picking the brain of the principal on a daily basis about instruction, start now. The principal has been placed in the position for several reasons. The two most important reasons are general leadership abilities and more importantly, instructional leadership skills. The principal was hired by the school board with the blessing of the superintendent in the belief that he or she is more than capable of leading instruction and implementing district initiatives. Collaborating with the principal provides ideas and strategies to carry out with the departments that the assistant principal supervises or with the entire staff. Participating in articulation activities and games with the principal will provide further information and practice for working with the departments. Practice what you plan to teach.

If there are no opportunities to lead instruction or to be placed in an instructional leadership situation, collaboration with the principal about instruction is needed. Some schools may have different hierarchies or management divisions that keep an individual from instruction. The principal may need to know that the assistant principal is interested and well versed in the instructional role. Collaboration builds a comfort level for the principal when making decisions about the assistant principal leading instruction. The ability to sit down and participate in a rich and descriptive discussion about instruction shows the principal that background knowledge needed to begin leading instruction has been developed and one is ready to move to the next level—working with and leading teachers.

First Steps at Leading Instruction

Drafting a professional development proposal and corresponding presentation for the principal to review prior to an actual presentation to staff is a good way to get started. Review it several times and practice it beforehand so that it is presented intelligently and then follow up on any suggestions and changes. An awkward presentation will reduce the effectiveness of a well-thought-out plan. Generally speaking, this probably will not be the process every time there is an idea for professional development, but it is a good way to get started. As confidence builds and presenting improves, the principal may just review the presentation and encourage additional presentations.

If the principal recognizes the assistant principal's ability to lead instruction, confidence in the assistant principal begins to build and extensive scrutiny of the assistant principal's work may subside with time and with success. However, being awkward and making mistakes in front of the whole faculty could be a downfall for both the assistant principal and for the principal, so it is best to follow the "practice makes perfect" motto. The assistant principal should solicit feedback from the principal after presentations, and after interactions with students, staff, and parents. Ask for it. Do not wait for the principal to approach. Focus on the important things, the important situations. Find a niche. Where are the gaps? Where can a difference be made? Self-assess with a global vision. Making a difference by filling these gaps will ensure a credible instructional leadership role.

Much to Do After the Training

Keep in mind that instructional leadership is not just about training staff, although it is one component of instructional leadership, it is only the beginning. For instructional leadership to be truly meaningful and effective after the initial training, followup, support, and clarification are needed. This part—followup, support, and clarification—will be the biggest challenge for an assistant principal leading instruction as it requires a great amount of time, time that is often yielded to managerial issues. The district calendar has built-in professional development days that allow for training, but days to followup on such training have to be blended into the assistant principal's schedule. There are many things that will pull the assistant principal away from followup, support, and clarification. However, the further apart these supports are, the less meaningful the initial training becomes. Think about all the time and effort that was put into the preparation of a staff development session, including the planning and actual presentation of material. Now think about all of it going out the window if there is no followup to the training. This is not a wise investment of time.

As time goes by without follow up, so does all of the hard work that led up to the implementation of the training. Additionally, this lack of support will follow the next time teachers are trained, making it very difficult to implement a desired goal. Time management is an important leadership trait and must always be kept in mind so that time is budgeted for followup on the training. Time management strategies are very important. It will be necessary to reflect on the daily schedule and the operations of the building to see where time can be restructured. Just remember that it takes more time to go back and correct a problem than it takes to ensure it is done correctly in the first place.

Freeing Up Time to Support Instruction

Collaborating with the principal can generate ideas about how to best manage time so that the assistant principal can follow up and support teachers. The principal may have ideas as to who can cover some of the lunch block supervision or who can process some of the minor infraction notices (e.g., tardies, skipping, and minor disruptive behavior) that seem to multiply on the desk so that time is freed up for instructional purposes. The principal may be able to suggest how to get assistance with some of the special education meetings or work on getting general education teachers flextime so that they are willing to attend these meetings past their contract time after school. This allows time to observe instruction during the school day. Some of these duties could be incorporated into internship hours for those teachers completing administrative degrees or by those teachers who already hold an administrative degree and would like opportunities to expose themselves to administrative experiences. Admittedly, some of these duties may seem rote and boring, it is important for aspiring administrators to see that the job is not all glamorous, but necessary for the school to conduct its instructional business.

Unfortunately, if the principal is unwilling or cannot free up some time with the suggestions I mentioned, then it becomes necessary to budget time to spend in the classrooms. Do not let this be a deterrent or a reason not to get involved with instruction. I believe most principals will carve out an instructional piece for assistant principals because it is what is best for students. Some states and school systems are developing positions such as school administration managers (SAMs) who free principals of many of the administrative responsibilities that pull them from instructional leadership. Christina Samuels (2008) reported in an *Education Week* article about SAMs:

> Investigators who shadowed principals for a week showed that a crush of managerial duties allowed them to spend only a third of the day—or less—on tasks that involved interaction with students and teachers. And often, the contact was too short and unfocused to lead to real instructional improvement. (p. 1)

It will be interesting to see if this idea is helpful and spreads throughout school districts across the country. It seems to be an excellent idea that, if supported by resources, will assist administrators in their instructional goals and school systems in meeting the rising NCLB benchmarks. There are already many similar setups across the country, such as deans, disciplinarians, and administrative assistants.

Be mindful, however, that principals are not in the business to help free up one's schedule to make it possible to complete paperwork or perform additional operational duties. Remember what I said earlier about not being considered for instructional responsibilities if operational duties cannot be accomplished. Principals have operational duties too, so they will have no sympathy. Making life easier would be nice, but it surely is not the goal; ensuring quality instruction is. If a request to free up some time is based on genuine instructional initiatives, the principal will probably agree because it is paramount to building a better and a stronger school and supporting the principal's instructional vision for best educating students.

The Value of Informal Collaboration

Collaboration with the principal does not always require formal meetings. It can be a hallway discussion, a quick pop in to each other's office, or some chatter while supervising a ball game or other activity. These are all valuable times to converse and to reflect on the direction of the school. Sometimes it is even better because these situations are more relaxed and the mind is clearer. Scheduling formal meetings is important and necessary, but the informal meetings can be just as valuable and can provide clarity to the formal meetings as they often allow for brainstorming of ideas that may not come under the pressures or time constraints of a formal meeting. We often jot down some of our best ideas at extracurricular events so we do not forget to revisit these ideas later.

Formal meetings can sometimes get bumped as a result of unexpected events that happen throughout the day or after school. If a bus were to get into an accident or return to school because of a fight, the meeting would get pushed back or postponed. Who knows when such a meeting could be rescheduled, especially if multiple administrators with conflicting schedules are involved? Quite often, many of our administrative team meetings happen by chance rather than by scheduling. Therefore, although it is a priority that formal meetings about instruction occur, they cannot always be guaranteed because of unforeseeable circumstances, so take full advantage of those unplanned discussions.

Beyond the professional side of collaboration with the principal is the personal side. Many hours are spent together because of the nature of the job. A great deal of confidential information (e.g., personnel issues) is exchanged and expected to remain private. It is possible to spend more time with the principal, at least during certain weeks, than with a spouse and children. There has to be a bond and a high level of trust as with a good friend, but on a professional level. Basically, this bond will allow administrators to work as a unified team and this is important for the students, the staff, the parents, and the community to observe. Without this discernible bond, stakeholders will try to split the team to get what they want (divide-and-conquer strategy). If the bond is strong, there is no place to drive the wedge and split the team. Please understand that I am not promoting an "us" versus "them" mentality; rather, I am advocating the need for a unified administrative team to effectively run a school, regardless of the members' different personalities and leadership styles.

Appropriately Venting to the Principal

Collaborating with the principal on a personal level allows time to express frustrations up the professional ladder because venting down to those who are supervised is toxic to the school, its mission, and its ability to become better and stronger. If it is okay for the administration to be negative it is okay for the staff to be negative, and thus for the students to be negative. This is not the type of leadership that moves schools forward. The assistant principal is faced with many negative issues and stressors on a daily basis and being able to talk it out and be heard is effective. Just remember that there is a big difference between whining and complaining versus venting and then brainstorming for practical solutions to the problem or to the frustration.

We have always had a golden rule at the schools in which I have worked: It is fine for a person to have a complaint, a concern, or an issue, but there must also be a potential solution to solve the problem. This takes a little more effort and contemplation, but is more positive than just telling other people what all the problems are around the school. These people are easy to identify. It is important that potential solutions are valued or else people will stop coming up with them or focus on the problem. We do not want people to hide problems from us because we cannot be aware of everything. Problems without proposed solutions tend to create frustration and hostility which usually result in a blame game. Solutions tend to create better and stronger people and schools because they promote teamwork. Having a positive attitude and working in a positive environment is much better for everybody and students ultimately benefit.

Do not vent all the time, only about major issues or concerns. Crying wolf too many times will be damaging when a wolf is really seen. Choose your battles carefully. Fighting every battle presented in educational administration would cause exhaustion and an inability to win the war, the war to help children succeed. The principal has a hard job too, and is a great resource for conversation and venting, but the principal cannot be a sponge for all of the problems. Remember that principals have their own set of problems. Sometimes just some laughing and joking are the best medicine for ailing administrators.

The assistant principal will need to relax a little, go home, take a walk, watch some television, read a book (not about education), and give it some time (sleep on it) when things get very stressful. This is not easy, but it often helps. Each day is a new start and a chance for a better day than the previous one. Without this attitude, the days will be long and burdensome with no light at the end of the tunnel and this will become progressively worse with time. The principal is a person to whom to vent but not when there has been a minor issue or a bad day. A principal is a boss, friend, and colleague all rolled up into one package, but these roles must not be abused or taken for granted.

Talking to the Principal About Career Aspirations

Good collaboration with a principal is important for the future of the assistant principal's career as well. Sharing with a principal what short- and long-term career goals the assistant principal has is very important. Remember that the principal was once in the same shoes and it is a good idea to pick the principal's brain as to how he or she got to the principalship. Additionally, the principal may have future plans about his or her own career and how he or she intends to get there in the next several years. If the principal does not know the assistant principal's career plans, the principal has no way of helping the assistant principal meet those professional goals. Do not just tell a principal about career plans, focus on executing the plan.

Many people have goals, but fail to develop an execution plan to meet such goals and may need help developing this plan. Plans may involve additional graduate school courses, training, and opportunities to develop as an assistant principal through professional growth opportunities (e.g., summer school principal, or specific instructional leadership roles). Such opportunities may include those things that go above and beyond the job description of the assistant principal. It may include school finance, master scheduling, additional instructional leadership opportunities, and serving on committees pertinent to the principalship.

Principals are the ones who can help an individual gain an array of experiences, but only if they know that there is an interest. Without this knowledge, the principal may presume that he or she is dumping extra work on the assistant principal and may be hesitant about doing so. After all, they have been in similar shoes and know the amount of work faced each day. The principal is the link between the assistant principal and the key central office personnel who make the hiring decisions. The larger the division, the less chance an assistant principal has of being known to those who make the hiring decisions regarding principals. It is important to be known. Do not just rely on the fact that a body of work will speak for itself. The person could very well be one of the best assistant principals in the district, but that does not necessarily get an individual's name outside the schoolhouse walls or illustrate a body of work to those not in the building.

Assistant principals need their principal to share with the directors and assistant superintendents the things that the assistant principal is doing in the building. This will set the person apart from other candidates because of tested and proven leadership abilities. These good things should start with sound instructional leadership but should also paint a complete picture of an ability to lead and to work under pressure and make decisions in order to run a school successfully. These suggestions are true regardless of career aspirations. There are many career assistant principals who are great leaders and are the backbone of many schools who I deeply admire and respect.

Do the Job Well, Then Ask for Support

It is important for you to be a great assistant principal for the principal to start advocating for you at the central office. Bear in mind, when the principal endorses a person, their name is attached to that endorsement. Thus their reputation regarding judging character and future leaders is at stake. This is not personal. It is a business and should be treated as such. Remember that we are working with children and there is no going back when mistakes are made. Running a school while ensuring the safety and the learning of hundreds to thousands of students is one of the toughest jobs a person can ever have. Think about all the issues, concerns, and potential problems that can arise each and every day that require sound decision making. For a principal to support one's hiring as a principal means that there is trust with one of the single most important responsibilities that exist—children.

Do not put a principal in an uncomfortable or awkward situation when it comes to promotion. If you believe you are doing a superb job and are deserving of such an endorsement, then tell the principal and explain the reasons why. One's body of work should speak for itself, but a voice will strengthen it. Give the principal an escape route to say that working on a few more things is necessary. Do not be angry or hurt with such a response. It is not personal. Remember what I said about the principal putting his or her reputation on the line as he or she advocates for you. The job is to take the advice from the person currently doing the job and run with it, make the improvements.

Ask principals for their help with a résumé or career vita and the identified areas in need of improvement. Show the principal that improvement is possible and that the advice is much appreciated. It is similar to having somebody proofread a written paper for mistakes after it has been read many times. Something may be missed, but a fresh set of eyes with a different perspective can help improve the quality of the document and correct mistakes. Turning sour and wearing disappointment on one's sleeve only impacts children negatively. If children are impacted negatively, the person looks bad. Looking bad will never get that endorsement from the principal.

On the contrary, if the job is not being done, do not ask the principal for help! Many principals have worked extremely hard and for many years to get to where they are and expect that a person will work just as hard or harder to reach such a point. A principal will probably start talking about the principalship and encouraging the person to apply for vacancies inside or out of the district if the principal believes that the person is ready and has the essential skills. If this happens, the assistant principal needs to be prepared to discuss it and to move forward, to make a decision. As an experienced assistant principal this may mean that the principal thinks that you will be ready in a few years or sooner. If you are only a year or two into the job, then the timeline might be a little longer, but it does not have to be. Some principals may want to keep the assistant principals that they have trained and molded to accomplish the goals of the school as a team. This is certainly understandable and something to consider when asking for their endorsement.

There is no way that a principal can offer everything or expose a person to everything needed to be prepared for the principalship, but one can certainly get a good taste of what is to come. There is so much on-the-job training that comes with the position that a person has to develop a set of skills that can be applied to each new situation that arises. This will not be in a book or a principal's file until it actually happens. Once it does, previous knowledge and skills can be applied from past situations to the new situation. Take physical and mental notes and refer to them should something similar occur in the future. This is on-the-job training and the best thing that can be done is to apply previous knowledge to each new situation that arises. This is done every day in the court of law as judges and justices use past court decisions to apply decisions to unique, but similar cases.

Principals Do not Like Surprises

Although the focus has been on collaborating with the principal to become a better instructional leader, it is not the only focus of collaboration. In the field of educational administration, surprises are not usually a good or welcomed thing. I would venture a guess that a principal usually does not like surprises, at least as they relate to school. Therefore, it is best that the principal be made aware of anything contentious that is known that may cross his or her desk, such as issues dealing with students, discipline, parents, teachers, coaches, and the facility. Basically, this is anything known that a principal is going to get a call about or things that could make it to the media in this age of quickly disseminated digital information. This is not to say that the principal should be a micromanager of the assistant principal or that the principal has to know every single detail of all encounters. It is actually quite the contrary. If the principal were a micromanager, no decisions would be made without consultation. An individual would simply carry out the order given per each unique situation.

That the principal has given the assistant principal autonomy with the position warrants the respect of keeping the principal informed of any happenings. If the principal is not informed, it makes it more difficult to support these decisions as the only information the principal is receiving is from the reporting party. Additionally, a phone call to the ill-informed principal by the superintendent seeking answers about a disgruntled parent's phone call will create havoc. Trust me. No one would want to receive the followup phone call from a principal should this happen.

The principal being caught off guard is not a good thing and tracking down the assistant principal for information that the principal should have already been informed of is worse. Because the principal is typically the first level of an appeal process, the principal should have the full portfolio of information with documentation (e.g., statements, photographs, physical items, and videotape clips) and the fact that an appeal is being made should not be a surprise. The principal does not have time to micromanage the assistant principal's affairs or to stop by each day to see if there are any revelations that the principal should be prepared to handle. Collaborating with the principal will create a daily dialogue that will make both aware of what is going on in the building.

Sometimes, appeals go straight to the principal bypassing the assistant principal. However, I will say that the assistant principal will get a feel for this based on how well a conversation goes with the parent. Any time I sense that a parent is frustrated, upset, or in disagreement with me, I report it to my principal, even if the parent is polite about it. It is just something that is sensed. The expectation is that the principal will seek information for clarification and gather any additional documentation that may have been collected, as well as the assistant principal's input. Certainly, no one would want the principal to listen only to the other party and then render a decision, so dialogue is important.

Proactive Communication with the Principal

Communication is a two-way street. Do not hesitate to talk things over with a principal. Only the well-informed can make informed decisions. Keep the principal well-informed. This does not mean that the principal will always agree and he or she may offer advice on how a situation could have been handled better or may even ask for a decision change before an appeal ever occurs. This is important because it empowers the assistant principal, not the parent. Collaboration does not mean that agreement with the principal's decision is guaranteed, but the principal is the person who has to answer to the stakeholders (i.e., parents, superintendent, and school board) and stands accountable at the end of the day. Do not take this personally. The principal has to answer to many people and may make an unpopular decision, but a decision that he or she feels is appropriate for the given situation and in the best interests of everybody. Being in the hot seat is a tough job and we do not know how we will handle it until we are actually in that situation. Thus it is best not to make quick judgments.

Collaboration is more about making the principal aware and learning by conversing. If the principal overturns or lightens a decision and the response is negative, the responder loses, not the principal. As long as the principal gives an explanation for the decision, use it as a learning experience and move on to the next development. It is similar to not agreeing with a play that a coach calls in a big game in a crucial situation. Do not question the play as that is not the player's job. The job is to execute it, make it happen, and move on regardless of the result, because there is always the next play or the next issue. Learn from the situation and move on while remembering that every situation is different and is a new learning opportunity. Maintain the relationship with the principal and keep moving forward. Take the personal side out of tough decisions. The assistant principal will have some tough ones to make as well and will want to be supported (usually by teachers)—do not forget that! Do not get stalled on petty differences of opinion. If this happens enough times, there will be a stigma attached to you as not being a team player and as someone who cannot accept constructive criticism—not typical characteristics of a leader.

8

Building a Better
and Stronger School

Great schools have to begin with great instructional leadership and this is where the assistant principal comes into the picture. In *Leadership for Differentiating Schools and Classrooms* (2000), Carol Ann Tomlinson and Susan D. Allan pose a very thought-provoking question: "Do our current [instructional] practices make learners more independent or more dependent" (p. 2)? This is a question for which the answer must be, regardless of costs, the catalyst for improving schools in America and, perhaps, everywhere in this world. Students may be ill-served until school leaders and educators begin to answer this pressing question. Beyond answering this question, action will be needed to make the changes necessary to avoid ill-serving the children. Indeed, building a better and a stronger school is a tremendous challenge. But, it is a challenge worthy of the time and the energy that is required for mastery. If we want to have great schools, we must first begin the journey by answering the question posed by Tomlinson and Allan and then take action. With the flattening world (see Friedman, 2005), students must become independent, critical thinkers, and educators must stop being the gatekeepers of knowledge.

Jim Collins (2001) tells us that good is the enemy of great and that we do not have great schools, first and foremost because we have good schools. This is true of business, government, and individual attainment. In other words, good is the enemy of many things. Let us face it, a pretty good life is not so bad. Sometimes an individual has accomplished more than he or she ever thought was possible. He or she may have assets never dreamed possible compared to their parents' financial situation and what he or she had growing up. However,

101

the problem lies in this very form of contentment for which we have varying degrees. Realizing and obtaining full potential is often lost in comfort, convenience, and a lack of motivation, or a fear of failure. Being good is about being comfortable and being comfortable is about not wanting to change or having the motivation to change. Not wanting to change or to improve is the roadblock to greatness. It is mediocrity.

A Better and Stronger School

A good starting point is a discussion of what a better and a stronger school is and my answer is based on my experience as an assistant principal. There is no single response because many factors are involved. But answering the question does have potential for pedagogical exploration. It is quite clear that poorly performing schools are taking drastic steps to become better and for obvious reasons. It would seem to make sense that schools that are good should be taking drastic steps to be great and for obvious reasons. Both groups should be striving for continuous school improvement. It is agreed that one group has more at stake than does the other. One group is fighting for survival whereas the other is near the top of the food chain. Obviously, the motivation and the risks for the two schools are quite different and yet they are the same.

One group is trying to survive attack from the parents, the community, and a possible state takeover, whereas the other is camouflaged from scrutiny by its mere goodness, many pleased stakeholders, and minimal discontent. This is not an attack on either good schools or poorly performing schools. It is, however, a discussion of the level of motivation rooted within each type of school to improve and to change, to become better. How about the motivation of great schools? What are great schools doing to remain great compared to what good schools are doing to remain good? How does this compare with great teams, great organizations, or great companies? What kind of school is desired for a child to attend? These are all pertinent questions to ponder. Continue to bear in mind the Jim Collins' comment noted earlier as to why we do not have great schools. No matter the type of school, there is always room for improvement. This room for improvement is based on the fact that students change each year so we need to change each year or we will lose more and more of them with time.

Better and Stronger One Person at a Time

Building a better and stronger school is not an easy task nor is it an overnight episode. Sometimes it can be as slow as one person at a time. It means change and we know that change is a process, not an event. It takes time (years) and patience. Furthermore, change requires a rationale followed by action and then buy in from all of the stakeholders involved in a child's education. Being a good school can make this a rather difficult task. After all, good schools seem to be keeping most of the stakeholders happy and with the stakeholders happy, there is seemingly no pressure or motivation to be better and stronger. With very little voice, those few stakeholders who view it differently are hard to hear. Are these the children who are truly being left behind?

What constitutes a good school should probably be added to this discussion as well. At first glance, the answer seems quite obvious. It is probably something like a school that is safe, has genuine teachers who are highly qualified, and has performed well on state assessment standards along with surpassing the *No Child Left Behind* (NCLB) requirements. Of course, there are other factors such as sound athletic programs, school spirit, positive activities, and arts programs that are all important to a good school. All of these things make a good school, but who determines if a school is good? If a parent's child is not doing well academically and is not passing the state-required tests for graduation or promotion then the argument that the school is not good may be a valid one. This is not to say that every child will succeed in any school (poor, good, or great), but the expectation is that every child should succeed or should have the opportunity, support, and resources to do so. Great schools are focusing on the students who are being left behind, but that is not their only focus. There is also a focus on students who are doing well but should or could be doing better. Not pushing the good students can be just as much of a disservice as leaving the struggling students behind.

The Principal Cannot Do It All

The principal cannot be the only instructional leader in the school. The load is simply too great for one person to carry all of the time. The principal may set the focus and share the instructional mission, but it has to be carried out by many others through collaboration. Yes, ultimately the principal has to make sure it gets done, but with the assistance of a team. The assistant principal is the next level of leadership in the building and must be in tune with the principal when it comes to all forms of leadership, but most particularly, instructional leadership. Strong instructional leadership is needed to develop a better and a stronger school. It will not happen by itself or through wishful thinking. It takes serious action and on a daily basis. Remember that the mission must have teeth. Strong instructional leadership is needed to help struggling students succeed and to make good students great.

All of the chapters in this book are ingredients in building a better and stronger school. All of the chapters deal with the assistant principal's role in building a better and stronger school, whether managerially or instructionally or both. The assistant principal should have a significant role in the leadership required to improve a school. Yes, the assistant principal has many roles and a very extensive job description that cannot really be explained in words. The job must be experienced to have any notion of its intensity; it must come in the form of on-the-job training. Just a walk down the hallway can spell disaster for an assistant principal's agenda for the day. However, the job can be very rewarding, but it has to be made rewarding. An assistant principal has to be positive, and mentally forget about the negative. I have found that just holding a school together (some days this all I can hope for) is quite stressful and frustrating, but when everything clicks, it is inspirational. Assistant principals have to have a short memory when it comes to the bad things so that they can remain positive.

Separating Operational
Issues from the Mission

There is no reward for maintaining what is already in place or what had already existed upon arrival. The assistant principal has to create the positive change. He or she has to be the change agent, the improvement agent. Rewards are not found in the operational side of the job description, although there are some dividends that do occur in this area, making this area important. Do not get me wrong, operations are an imperative ingredient in the building of a better and a stronger school and should not lack any focus nor be overlooked. Just be careful not to put all of the eggs into one basket, the managerial basket, and forget about other important ingredients in the recipe for success. I have found this to be an unintended trap at all three schools in which I served.

Often times, the operational issues come with many urgent labels, trapping the administrator into the nonacademic side of the job to meet mandated deadlines. It becomes a trap because these deadlines usually require immediate attention and often require time, resources, and paperwork, which often draws one away from instruction. The best advice that I can give is to take care of the immediate needs of the situation and complete the paperwork after students have left the building for the day, prioritize when possible. This may mean that notes need to be jotted down, or thoughts recorded so that paperwork accurately reflects the incident or issue when later completed. Just keep in mind the principal does not like surprises so it is important to inform the principal of the plans per the situation if it is necessary. Moving some paperwork to after school hours should provide some time to get into the classrooms for at least an adequate amount of time.

Many hours will still need to be spent on particular nonacademic issues, but buying just an hour for instruction is better than nothing at all. A fight between two students can be very time-consuming to investigate and to administer appropriate disciplinary action. It is very important that the assistant principal gets all of the facts correctly as parents will want to know them, and perhaps local law enforcement, depending on the nature and severity of the fight along with possible retaliation from friends. This may mean hours of interviewing witnesses, collecting statements, and viewing security camera tapes for proper documentation. Furthermore, reports are needed from the school nurse as to the extent of the injuries, statements from the students involved in the fight, completing infraction notices, and contacting the parents to explain the incident and the consequences and possibly meeting with those parents in person. Typically, if everything goes quickly and smoothly, it is at least a two-hour process or longer. This, of course, is two hours or more that were not on the agenda, but now have been unexpectedly lost.

Making Good Days Busy Days

How is lost time recovered? The truth is that it is not! The assistant principal has to learn ways to get back chunks of lost time, but not all lost time, because that is impossible. It could be that it is necessary to stay a little later that day or come in a little earlier the next morning. I may take a working lunch or no lunch at all—not my recommendation because it is not healthy and can become a habit, but a way to get back some lost time on occasion, especially if it is not possible to stay late or come in early. The good news is that there tends to be some balance in the position. There are good days and there are bad days. Although the bad days may set a person back and seem overwhelming, the good days are an opportunity to catch up or even get ahead on some of the duties. This balance may not be on a weekly basis or even a monthly basis. I have found that the good and bad come in clusters, but neither lasts forever, although sometimes it seems like it.

We are familiar with the "calm before the storm" saying and must always be preparing for that storm just as we would in the event of a real storm. Although this may not be the best analogy, it is one that should be heeded. We have to make good days just as busy and crazy as bad days to create balance. By this I mean that when assistant principals are having those rare days with no interruptions or distractions, it has to be taken advantage of as much as possible. These days must be extremely productive and instructionally focused, realizing that the next day may not present such an opportunity. Get out into the classrooms and stay there for the entire day or as much of the day as possible. If the assistant principal is absolutely needed, he or she will be called on the radio with the specific information. Check in with the secretary for "hot topics" during class changes or at lunch.

Stopping by the office during instructional time is a sure means of pulling the assistant principal from the classroom as there is always something that he or she could be doing, but may not be urgent. Unfortunately, what is considered urgent varies based on the person delivering the information to the administrator. Not stopping by the office is easier said than done because one quickly realizes the amount of work that can pile up for after school and thus lengthen the already long day for the assistant principal. However, some of the work that can be deferred to after school is the kind of work that keeps administrators out of classrooms during the day and goes against the mission of building a better and stronger school. Thus good days are a great opportunity to catch up for the time that was lost on bad days, but realize that good does not mean easy. It does mean that these are days to do what one is really passionate about—visiting classrooms to see instruction. I believe that assistant principals will find these busy days rewarding and that they will go by quickly. The key is learning how to keep the growing managerial duties out of mind while in the classrooms. Usually, I get so involved with the lesson and the students that I forget about everything else. Do not worry, reality comes back quickly.

Beating Stress

Getting into classrooms and being around students in a positive atmosphere is the best medicine for an ailing assistant principal. Busy days do not necessarily mean bad days. However, days that pull the assistant principal away from instruction and expose him or her to negativity can be taxing on the attitude. Too much exposure to or focus on the negative can have dire consequences on school improvement and on the administrator. Think about any life situation when a person was stressed or distracted and the impact that it had on the person and the family. More than likely, it kept the individual from doing anything else 100%; it had a major impact on focus, attitude, and mood. Presence may have been there physically, but mentally he or she was elsewhere thinking about the stressor, and thus did not give a best effort. Stress is a topic that has been well-researched. Anxiety, depression, nervous tension, and memory loss are some symptoms that come to mind. None of these things are good for the personal health of an administrator, or their family, or their school. Creating balance is the key to success. Taking good days and turning them into productive, busy days can make the assistant principal feel better mentally and this will help assist in giving it the best for all situations encountered.

We work in such a mentally stressful environment that staying healthy mentally has a positive impact on our physical health. Yes, the job does have some physical demands that can make a person tired and in need of a break from time to time, such as weekends, holidays, or personal days. For me, most (not all) of this is nothing that cannot be fixed with a good night's sleep or a power nap. Mental stress can be very taxing and lead to sleepless nights, which can lead to vulnerability to sickness due to low immunity, which leads to low productivity or absences. Taking care of mental health by reducing stress is critical for survival as an assistant principal.

Because stress is something that can leave work with a person and follow him or her home, it must be managed vigilantly. It cannot be eliminated but it must be managed and controlled. One big stressor for the assistant principal is leaving work everyday knowing that there is so much still to be completed and also knowing that tomorrow will only add to the incomplete list, compounding the problem to a point where there is no light at the end of the tunnel. This concern of compounding incomplete tasks can lead to concerns about job security, an additional stressor, making a person feel like he or she is not doing the job. For this I say to think about it this way. If stress causes physical illness and this illness keeps a person out of work for a definite period of time, the work will never be caught up and the stress will be further exacerbated. Work hard to do the best possible each and every day and let it go (as much as possible) when walking out the door. Do not work to the point of collapse. Work hard, but smart.

This relates back to my discussion on taking good days and turning them into busy days. Busy and bad are two different things in the context of educational administration. I can be busy doing the things that I really enjoy, which in this case (while at school) is interacting with the students and teachers in the classrooms or collaborating with staff. This can make for very busy days, but days of positive and refreshing fun, days to follow up on instruction, and to support teachers in their efforts to improve instruction. These types of days take away from the stress and the negativity because a person really gets to see the work as an assistant principal come to practice. Spending time in the classrooms opens eyes as to how all the different things being done feed directly into the learning process that takes place in the classrooms. This is the cycle of school improvement and it is great to experience. Just be sure to take time to recognize greatness and share praise when deserved.

Seeing the Vision in Action

While the credit should go to teachers, students, and parents, it is very inspiring to sit in a classroom where students are actively engaged and learning and be able to say mentally that because of all the things I do, this can take place. This is the result of my hard work. It really does come to fruition, it really does matter. I can see the vision. This is important because the assistant principal can quickly fall into a quagmire of negativity from constant exposure to infraction or discipline notices, which focus only on the negative. It is a job with so many challenges that we often overlook the good things to prepare for the next challenge. Sure it is a great thing when an administrator can work with a student who is a discipline problem so that their behavior improves, but that may take just as much, if not more time, than many classroom visits. Again, I am always happy when I can get a child to change his or her behavior and be successful, but I would rather prevent the behavior in the first place, if I can, through helping teachers with active student engagement in the classroom via sound academic management strategies.

For student achievement to be at an acceptable level or higher, many things have to come together to create a successful recipe. I do not want to generalize, but for purpose of being specific I will say that engaging instruction, valid assessment, and classroom management must be the cornerstone of a successful teacher's classroom. Keep in mind that all of these elements are intertwined and do not stand alone or in a particular order of importance. Engaging instruction can eliminate many behavior problems and make the assistant principal's job easier in the long run by reducing discipline notices. But, administrators have to get out into classrooms to clarify, guide, and support the type of instruction that they desire. A well-known leader in my school division often says, "You have to inspect what you expect." This is true and straight to the point. Imagine where many successful companies would be without quality control on their assembly lines.

Prioritize Problems, Do Not Ignore Them

The job requires much time and energy; the question is does the assistant principal want to spend the time and energy doing mostly positive or mostly negative things? The question is not as simple as it seems. Although the answer may seem obvious, it is not. This is because although we want to spend our time focusing on instruction, the negative issues always seem to demand our immediate attention for a variety of reasons (e.g., deadlines, parental pressure, or political rapport). This is a culture that has to be broken and a new one with better priorities created, with students in mind. We have been stuck in the past for far too long and it is time to move forward, to progress, just as the hunters and gatherers once did. Some of how we prioritize our time we have control over and some of it is part of the organizational structure for running schools that has long been in place.

Better and stronger schools do not ignore problems; instead, they prioritize problems that can negatively impact the instructional mission of the school. The focus has to be on instruction and student learning while stomping out those issues that will have a negative impact on this focus or that undermine school goals. Building better and stronger schools is like the parts of a well-oiled machine working together as one unit. It is about establishing a culture of sound instruction and learning where everybody in the building knows this and is on the same page. It is about a team. It is automatic. Students should expect and get consistency no matter where they are in the building. It is not about a group of staff members working in isolation and only being concerned with their piece of the pie. This is why I wrote such an extensive section on relationship building among teachers. It is so critical for success!

It's About the Students, Not Us

Building a better and stronger school is not an easy thing. The key is to get started, do something, and start improving today because every positive thing we do, no matter how little, can help students. Do not let the fact that it is a long process that may not be seen to the end (e.g., because of a promotion or a change of schools) be a deterrent. The bottom line is that school leaders have to do what is best for students. It does not matter if an individual will still be there or if someone else will be the replacement down the road and perhaps receive the credit for earlier grassroots efforts. It is about investing in the future that really matters, not who gets the accolades; that the school has become a great school and is developing productive citizens who can successfully compete in a globally competitive world. Knowing in our heart that we did great things for students is a much better reward than any accolade. Our accolades should lie within students and what they go on to do in the future, even if we never see them again after they walk across the stage at graduation.

Once school leaders move past the mentality of getting individual credit for accomplishments and move toward helping students succeed, the rewards of the job will be truly felt. This is a tough thing to do because school administrators are in a competitive position in which there may be a desire to move up the career ladder and a comparison of one school versus others could make a difference on how a person is viewed as an instructional leader. It is human instinct to be competitive and to want attention brought to the individual and to the school, especially when so much hard work has been done to help students succeed.

The true measuring stick for success at the end of the day is how students feel about their educational experience and the school environment. No reward, recognition, or advancement will ever make a person feel as good as a former student saying that he or she made a difference in his or her life or that he or she really appreciated the things that were done (by a teacher or by an administrator). Even though this may be years down the road (when students have had a taste of the real world), it still feels good. It is a gift that keeps on giving.

As communities change, so do students and thus so do the schools. We are required to be an ever-evolving profession to meet the diverse needs of the students who walk through our doors. Please understand that becoming a great school does not have a finish line that one crosses and thus is declared the champion or declared great. It is about being as great as possible every day. However, great schools do not ever let the goal of being great get out of sight; they keep moving closer and closer while bringing the students with them, hoping that the hard work will pay off for everybody. It is about being great every day in all aspects of education and letting the pieces fall where they may. Great schools are ones in which the mission is reflected in the day-to-day actions of the school and not just words posted on a wall that become ignored without action to give them life.

Concluding Remarks: An Extensive Book Summary

All of the information shared so far in this book is based on my own experiences of working in three high schools under the guidance of five different principals. Much time has been spent watching, listening, learning, and practicing. The components of leadership development are not just about learning what to do, but also what not to do. We know that we often learn more from our mistakes than from our successes. If a principalship is being pursued, do not be so hurried to get there that the benefits from the experience of being an assistant principal are lost. The job forces the assistant principal to be a manager, but it takes time to become a leader and with good reason.

My words are not intended to be the rule book for assistant principals, but more or less friendly and causal advice that assistant principals can take into consideration as they experience on the job training first hand. I am not claiming that I have all of the correct answers or that I have found the silver bullet for instant success. Truth be told, it is a difficult job. If it were easy, there would be many prospective assistant principals waiting to take over when the opportunity was presented, but this is not always the case. I am claiming what I have learned through my career as an assistant principal based on what has been successful and what has been unsuccessful, both for me as an individual and for the administrative teams and schools. Your success will depend on you. Jim Tressel, Ohio State University head football coach writes in his book *The Winners Manual*, "If a person measures his success by his inner satisfaction and the peace of mind that comes from knowing he did the best he was capable of doing for the group, he'll be able to gauge that success correctly" (p. 7). I hope you will be able to gauge your success this way.

Some suggestions within this book may work while others may not be of interest or within the current comfort zone. There will be a great deal of trial and error as the days go by. Again, there is no silver bullet because there is no target. Because excellence always moves, there is no destination which to aim or reach, but there are goals and timelines to guide. Striving to do great things for students each day should be the goal. The target keeps moving and the destination keeps changing, resulting in the development and the need for new and different ways to reach children. These new ways, of course, will be different from school to school across each district and state, but the core purpose will always remain the same—sound instruction supported by quality instructional leadership.

Although this book is based on my experiences to date, it is also based on my teaching experience, coaching experience, training, conferences attended, research, literature, collaboration with fellow assistant principals, instructional specialists, principals, and what I personally believe works based on all of the information that I have internalized. Experience alone is not enough to qualify a person as having knowledge in the area of instructional leadership, but it helps. Each day that we are on the job is another day of potential growth, but that does not necessarily mean that we learned anything. Experience can be defined in a variety of ways. Although time spent on the job is one definition and can be valuable, it has to be time that is used well. If so, experience is a powerful tool and the more there is, the better an administrator will be. It is safe to say that somebody with three years of experience may be more knowledgeable than someone with five years of experience if he or she has been really involved with all aspects of the job, and I mean totally emerged. Again, a person's body of work will speak for itself. People will work hard for and are motivated by leaders who set examples.

The more we practice instruction, the better we become at it because our experience has taught us what works and what does not. We learn what adjustments have to be made, what to expand upon, and what to eliminate so that our instruction is maximized. We cannot know these things without first having attempted to do them. Periodic or spotty instructional leadership does not result in valuable experience for the administrator or for the teacher. However, sustained instructional leadership that includes at least weekly (preferably daily) visits to classrooms along with followup collaboration is a start to gaining experience as an instructional leader. If weekly is not possible because of the job description, try once every two weeks. Regardless, do not go long periods of time without stepping foot into a classroom. The longer between visits, the harder it is to keep up with instruction.

My opinions and beliefs are not based only on what I have experienced as an assistant principal. Some things are learned by reading literature on instructional leadership. Others are based on professional development provided by the school board office or via professional conferences. Others, probably the most important, are based on professional dialogue with colleagues in different schools, and others are based on professional discussion within my own school walls. Factor in what I learned in my doctorate program courses along with the net-

working of fellow doctoral cohort members, ranging from superintendents to assistant principals, and I have learned quite a
bit as a school leader. All of these are important factors in determining the instructional leadership level of an assistant principal. Leaving any of these items out, short of the doctoral classes,
will not culminate in failure as an instructional leader, but may
prevent a person's maximum potential as a school leader from
being reached.

   I feel that anyone who can successfully do the things that
I have discussed is ready and deserving of taking the helm of
a building, if that is desired. A principal told me that a person
will never have that particular moment of waking up and deciding that this is the day. It is something that is just known
from working hard each day to be prepared when the opportunity arises. On-the-job training will be vital, but the foundation must be laid prior to taking over a school. Consequently,
assistant principals would be wise to learn everything they can,
even if it means going above and beyond their job description.

   Do not expect to have all of the answers, but be willing to
reach out to others to find such answers. The fact that an idea
or a solution is not original makes it no less important to implement if it will truly help students and teachers to succeed. Yes, it
is a very competitive business, and successfully implementing
new and innovative ideas is one way to advance a leadership
career. But, we must not sacrifice children along the way of a career path or self-interests. We must do what is best for children,
and if we do, our career path will take care of itself. This means
that assistant principals from all over a district, region, state,
and nation have to work together to help each other be better
and stronger leaders for the ultimate benefit of children and this
country's future. It is not about keeping great ideas a secret. We
are not the gatekeepers of information, but we should be the
crop dusters of knowledge. It is not about who gets credit for an
innovative idea. It is about what is best for children.

   An additional benefit to collaborating with fellow assistant
principals from the district is new information is learned by
teaching each other. Think about how much a person improves
at something when it is taught and explained to someone else.
Being able to teach reinforces the skill, making one better. Any

questions posed by the listener may spark new ideas as to how it can be improved and made stronger. Whether we think so or not, professional dialogue and brainstorming allow us to open our minds to things that we may not have thought of in the past. This is not to say that we are not creative or innovative as individuals, but it is to say that the strength of all of us working collectively is greater than the strength of all of us working in isolation or against each other. Additionally, it is more fun and more rewarding to work as a team. People like the interaction that comes with teamwork and appreciate an opportunity to break the barriers that isolation creates for assistant principals. Isolation weakens leaders, but collaboration and teamwork is the glue that holds a team together.

Administrators often call each other to discuss unique discipline, parental, and special education issues to gain insight and advice on how similar situations were handled at their respective schools. Why should this dialogue stop when it comes to instructional issues? Certainly picking up the phone and talking to a colleague about what kind of training he or she is giving to staff or how he or she is working with small groups of teachers to improve instruction should be an easy and exciting phone call. Perhaps, their schools have teachers who are doing some great things and the person is willing to share what is being done. Certainly, it would be easier and more fun than discussing stressful discipline, parental, and special education issues.

I have found that all assistant principals, no matter the grade level, have been more than helpful in any aspect of education, both operational and instructional. Yes, we are competitive with each other, but this benefits students as it makes us all work harder to outdo each other, but not at the expense of students. We know that we are a team of assistant principals and must work together to ensure that our isolation is not our demise in spite of the competitive nature. We must understand that we are individuals who make up a team, a school system.

Even though we are competitive, we are willing to share ideas because we know that the productivity of our future citizens is at stake. However, this competition is based on the fact that all schools have the same knowledge base and a level playing field when it comes to resources. Yes, the students may vary from school to school, but helping all students to succeed is the ultimate goal. There may be some ideas or programs that are unique to one school and this may be one of the things that a person does not want to share. My advice is to put it out there, share it with colleagues. Somebody may have a suggestion that could actually strengthen the program. Somebody may be able to make it better and stronger. Putting the work out there does not mean that the competition will get an edge, but offers a peer review of the work, constructive criticism. Just as college professors subject their publications to peer reviewed journals, school leaders should do the same with their work among their peers.

I anticipate that peer reviewing is what the next generation of leaders will be doing. I suspect that there will be open dialogue and collaboration with an opportunity to review each other's ideas, work, and data. Again this is what is best for students, but also plays a role in the success of the school district when it comes to state accreditation and NCLB standards for district schools collectively. Indeed, the district will have to pull its internal resources together to meet these demands and this task will be charged to all school-level leaders. After all, a school district which is not accredited puts a label on every school within that district in spite of individual school attainment. Meeting NCLB and state requirements alone is a slippery slope and once there is a slip, there is nobody there to help. For a person who openly and equally shares ideas and strategies, the slope is not so steep and has many plateaus to step onto for safety—colleagues who can help because they were not abandoned or because they were helped along the way.

Another point that I would like to discuss is the quality of the teacher leading the instruction in the classroom. This is not intended to shame teachers as I feel most have a big heart and want to do what is best for students and entered the profession for such reasons. However, this intent does not necessarily result in the desired outcome that stakeholders may have. Assistant principals are aware that no matter how much time we spend in the classrooms, it is not nearly close to the amount of time that teachers spend with students behind closed doors. While I have seen several administrators whom I would closely relate to Superman, none actually are (must be Kryptonite in the school building), and thus cannot be in every classroom every day for the full amount of class time.

Ultimately, the classroom doors shut and we have to hope with all of our being that teachers are doing the right thing—instructing with quality strategies from bell to bell as much as is possible in a given class period. Hope can only get a person so far though; the rest depends on action and execution. There has to be a mission, a vision, a climate, a culture, training, followup, and relationships that ensure that the ultimate goal, preparation for the real world, is fulfilled. If the administration can get buy-in through successful action from the people they lead and value their body of work, then hope is no longer needed because the core value of the school is that all teachers are on the same page and that this is what we do here. The teachers, much like players on a team, will push other teachers to do better by setting the bar so that the mission of the school is accomplished.

One of my principals would always say that the quality of a child's education should not be dependent on the luck of the draw when the students are scheduled into classes. After all, we are not playing cards or gambling, especially with the livelihood of our students. The principal would further explain that no matter which teacher the child has for an English class, the final results should be the same. The child should still be well prepared for the next level of English or college, or trade school, or the workforce, no matter what teacher he or she had. This is an extremely important and interesting point.

I know that the reader is already thinking about these types of disparities within his or her own school or from past experiences because this problem can occur. Think about the one teacher who is very demanding and the students are working so hard for that B grade while friends are with very little effort earning an A in the same subject in the other teacher's class. This is not fair and has several major implications that negatively impact both the child and the school. First it usually makes one teacher popular and the other less desirable. Second, it can also hurt the school's test scores as one teacher may significantly outperform the other. Third, students in one teacher's class may ultimately end up with a higher quality education and a better preparation for the next stage without the grade to reflect it. Do not get me wrong. I am not saying that the intent of any given teacher is to provide a lower-quality education to their students, but it can happen.

Unless all teachers are following the same set of musical notes, we will not be in tune with one another—some high, some low! There will always be slight differences, but the job as leaders is to narrow the gap in these differences. Leaders should not be taking away the autonomy or creativity, but should be asking for an equitable product. There are achievement gaps that have to be closed and students who have to be reached. Addressing these gaps should start with teachers who share a common subject. We know that without examining practices through collaboration, taking risks, and moving out of comfort zones that the gap will not close.

Are there answers to avoiding differences in quality? Yes. There are strategies that balance or help level the playing field for children. It all goes back to collaboration and fostering an environment in which teachers work together and throw out the competitive attitude. We have to move away from the attitude that if I am outperforming my colleague then the pressure is on him or her, not me, regardless of my test scores. This is counterproductive to teaching and to learning. Teachers are stronger as a team than in isolation, but can only learn this through opportunities to function as a team. We are naturally competitive and it does benefit students when we try our best, but we cannot hold back collaborative efforts in the process, because in education the means do justify the ends.

The good news is that there are many good teachers in America's classrooms. These good teachers have the opportunity to become great teachers, which is a benefit to their students. The question is how we as assistant principals guide good teachers down the path to becoming great teachers. Mike Schmoker (2006) noted in *Results Now* that in a 2001 study by Haycock and Huang it was discovered that the top teachers in a school have six times the impact than do the bottom teachers. This is quite a significant difference and leads one to ponder the question of who is teaching the children, and which students in a school get the top teachers and which students get the bottom teachers. It leads a person to understand that there is potentially a big difference in the quality of a child's education depending on who the teachers are, especially over a four-year period of time and just before an exit into the real world. The good news as stated by Schmoker is that

> Unprecedented improvements will merely require that we reorient the heart, the time, and the energy we now invest in failed models and activities into those commonsense actions and practices by teachers and leaders that would address the deficiencies—the opportunities—just delineated. (p. 19)

This quote from Schmoker should be positive and encouraging for those teachers who want to improve, to provide students a better future, and to make what they are doing each day more rewarding and less repetitive. Schmoker explains that the time and energy spent on failed models or on those models that used to work should now be reinvested into practices which meet the needs of all learners while moving away from the one size fits all approach. The best part is that the talent needed to improve lies within each school. Our own people are the experts, but we have to identify them and use them wisely. It costs nothing to improve, but it does require creativity in how we conduct our business, our process. As a country, we are no longer one size and hence need to provide a variety of sizes so that we clothe all of our students with a sound education.

I appreciate and have a great deal of respect for good teachers. I considered myself to be a good teacher, but not great despite my successful state test scores. However, I have come to realize that those test scores, which are so heavily emphasized, are not the only indicators of great teaching. Good teachers are the backbone of the American educational system and have been since the beginning of formal public education in America. The amazing thing about good teachers is that they are mostly successful without any interventions or coaching from school leaders, although they may need reinforcement and recognition to improve. Good teachers have a propensity to do what is best for students because they know in their hearts that it is the right thing to do. So, what is the difference between a good teacher and a great teacher? The answer is both encouraging and practical. It is within reach for good teachers. Initially, it does take some time and effort, but once the skills and resources are built, it becomes more natural and less time consuming. It becomes automatic.

The difference between good and great teachers is that great teachers have developed strategies to meet all or almost all learners in their classrooms via engaging and interactive instruction. They have tapped into that small percentage of students who are usually left behind in most other classrooms. They have found ways to motivate and to engage the students who normally would be behavior problems or mental dropouts. Great teachers still reach the same students whom the good teachers reach while pulling in those students who normally separate themselves from the rest because they cannot or will not do the work. Great teachers stretch the minds of those students who are already successful and prepared for school. Great teachers develop positive relationships with students. The question is how do they do this? It is not simple. It requires much time and a great amount of work. Great teachers are good collaborators, good researchers, and great consumers of instructional data.

Great teachers are interested in how their students learn, what their students' interests are (which helps them differentiate instruction when needed), and how formal and informal assessment data can be used to shape delivery of the content and enhance learning. Great teachers find ways to connect learning to student interests or to functional skills that can be used later in life. Great teachers develop lesson plans with other teachers, develop common assessments with other teachers, and discuss those assessment results with other teachers. Great instructors seek help from others, especially when their students struggle with a particular topic or lesson. Additionally, great teachers proactively seek constructive feedback in areas which they know they improvement. These are all components of a great teacher that can be accomplished by a good teacher. It is within their reach. It can start today.

The biggest part in the transition from a good to great instruction is taking the first step. Start a voluntary book club on student engagement or instructional strategies. Start a small collaboration team. Get a few teachers to develop a common lesson plan, a common assessment, an interest inventory, or differentiate a lesson. Have a small group of teachers analyze data. The assistant principal can start things and use some strong teachers to help. The assistant principal has to model expectations. The assistant principal can set the agenda, provide the data, and a small team can work together to establish benchmarks for the school year. It is okay to start small and let the success spread. There are teachers that want help, but may be afraid to ask. This way, they do not have to because they are part of a collaborative team.

Once the first step is taken, the momentum begins, confidence builds, and teachers begin to take ownership and leadership. This confidence is a symbiotic relationship for both the assistant principal and the teacher. As confidence grows, so does collaboration, and so does the number of students that are reached. I have personally seen collaboration start with as few as two teachers and then evolve gradually. It is really about a mentality. Great teachers have the mentality that they are going to use every resource possible to reach all of their students. Great teachers are confident and build upon that confidence. Great teachers are also realistic people in their goal setting. They realize that the chances of reaching every single student is a long shot, but they still go for it anyway. Great teachers do not let good students off the hook and try to reach the struggling learners in every way possible. It is important that teachers do not want to forget about the higher functioning students while focusing on the more needy students. While the more successful students may not slip through the cracks, they may be denied their potential learning ability.

Great teachers know that sometimes there are many variables outside their control (e.g., home life, drugs, depression, and gangs) that impact learning, but they still take the responsibility and undertake the challenge. Great teachers know that shooting for the stars means that they may fall on the moon, but that shooting for the moon may mean falling on the ground. Great teachers try to reach every student in any way with high expectations. They take mental notes and physical notes of what works and what does not. If they fail, they make changes, and know in their hearts that if they did not try they would never know. One thing that great teachers know is that when trying to reach all students there is no way most students will not be reached. Remember—shoot for the stars, not the moon.

Assistant principals along with the principal are responsible for fostering an environment that helps good teachers become great teachers and struggling teachers to become better teachers. Administrators should realize that the talent lies within the building, within the teachers, and use this as the catalyst for change. Relying on anything else could be a false sense of security. Jim Collins (2001) tells us in *Good to Great* that solutions from the outside can have a negative effect on the culture of improvement. True instructional leadership is about pulling the expertise from the teachers and placing it into a collaborative environment in which teachers instruct each other and learn from each other. Teaching is not restricted to the individual teacher's classroom. Teachers have to teach each other and administrators have to find ways to create teaching opportunities and learn from them.

Teaching and learning are lifelong skills that educators should practice and model for students. Administrators have to support this process in any way that they can (e.g., resources, training, time, compensation, and support) so that teachers do not feel as if their efforts are futile and unnoticed. Administrators have to be part of collaborative teams, but in a brainstorming and supportive capacity. Micromanaging is not needed and would only be counterproductive if exercised. But, quality control is required. Jim Collins (2001) addresses the issue of micromanagement this way: "The right people don't need to be tightly managed or fired up; they will be self-motivated by the inner drive to produce the best results and to be part of creating something great" (p. 42). Teachers who are vested in becoming great do not need or require somebody leaning over their shoulder causing undue stress. They need professional dialogue, clarification, support, and recognition when they succeed. They need a leader!

A great assistant principal must be a good listener and a person who is willing to be part of a discussion rather than leading and dominating the discussion when it comes to instruction. This can be difficult as it is often expected for the administrator to lead and to have all the answers. However, great school administrators realize and understand that they are not experts in every subject area and never will be, but they can be productive team members when it comes to instructional strategies which are applicable to all classrooms. They realize where the talent lies, within their own teachers who hold individual degrees, and who have tweaked their practices successfully through the years.

As leaders, administrators need to pull expertise out of teachers and put it into a usable format through collaboration. Mike Schmoker (2006) states it this way in *Results Now:* "The right kind of continuous, structured teacher collaboration improves the quality of teaching and pays big, often immediate, dividends in student learning and professional morale in virtually any setting" (p. 177). The results can be quick and immediate; it is the process of getting teachers aboard that needs constant and sustained leadership from administrators. The fact that immediate results for students can be achieved at no cost should be all the motivation a school leader needs to promote continuous teacher collaboration.

Administrators should be breaking the chains and locks off the gates of the information keepers for all to use. The best way to break these chains and locks is to foster a collaborative environment and to establish a mission that benefits children first. It is our role as administrators to have teachers take these chains and locks off willingly and to become leaders themselves. This may be a long and slow process, but one worthy to be undertaken. It may mean that it is a one-teacher-at-a-time process, and it may mean that some teachers have to go elsewhere if they are not willing to be part of the team. Be sure to replace these teachers with teachers who meet established selection criteria—those who are best for students and can put the mission into action. Of course, getting rid of ineffective teachers is a last resort after the administration has provided every support and resource possible to that teacher, but that teacher continues to pull the school down and other teachers clearly notice it and expect action. Teachers are well aware of the weak links in the chain and will be all too pleased to divulge this in a private conversation. Leaders must realize that a school will only be as strong as the weakest teacher.

Remember that there is a difference between a poor teacher who is struggling and really trying to improve and a poor teacher who shuns the help of the administration and colleagues. The same could be said for good teachers. It is all about a willingness to change behavior and ultimately attitude about what is best for children. None of the things that I have mentioned in this book ask a teacher to give up creativity or autonomy in the classroom, but improvement is not negotiable—not at all! Those things I have mentioned do require teachers to think about the best way to get information to children and to examine their data to see if it is working and make necessary adjustments. The administration has to drive this point home to teachers so that they understand that the administration is about improving instruction—not merely changing it. We are not in the business of change for the sake of change, but change for the sake of improvement.

Hopefully this book has helped beginning assistant principal's to look more clearly through the lenses of change in America's current public education system and make the appropriate adjustments to help all students achieve and succeed. Change is not a popular thing, but certainly carries enough momentum to knock a person over if he or she does not move with it. If the hunter and the gatherer refused to try farming, where would we be today? Changes in education are about building a better and stronger school without ever seeing the target that lies on the horizon. Building a better and stronger school is about realizing that students are changing and adapting to meet the needs of those changes. Adapting to these needs does not mean we abandon our past, but that we adapt to a new environment with appropriate changes. This means modifying some of the old skills and developing some newer ones. Change never gets easier and perhaps harder with time. No change is without risk, but risk equals reward and maintaining certain current practices could be a risk.

The good thing is that the kind of changes that are needed do not necessitate a complete abandonment of current pedagogical practices. The changes do not require that our teachers and our administrators be thrown out the door so that we can begin anew. However, change does mean that educators need to critically and frequently examine what they do, and make modifications to fit the learning needs of students. Yes, it will initially require a great deal of hard work. But the changes are vital. Change is a word that carries a negative connotation, but if we think of change in a positive manner we know it is really improvement—something positive.

An assistant principal may let people know that he or she does not have all of the answers, but is willing to work as a team to discover such answers. It is not required that a person has to be the genius or the micromanager; it is essential, however, to be the instructional leader—the one who fosters and supports the positive culture of school improvement. An assistant principal's position and title should be respected, revered, and understood, but always remember that the goal is for people to respect the individual as a leader. Most people will recognize the difficult position that the assistant principal has and see the challenges being faced daily when working unwaveringly for children. Lead by example. Model expected behaviors with a smile. Be a momentous element of the next generation of leaders!

Appendix

Managerial Duties of the Assistant Principal

Accident reports
Activities
Assemblies
Athletics
Awards
Back to school preparations
Bell schedules
Building Advisory Team/
 Staff Council
Buses and bus supervision
Business partners
Cafeteria
Child Protective Services
 (CPS)
Child Study meetings
Class/grade level meetings
Classroom and office assign-
 ments
Communications (all forms)
Conferences
Court
Crisis management/plans
Dances
Data analysis
Data collection
Difficult parents/disputes
Discipline
Discipline programs
Discipline reports

Documentation
Drills/Evacuations
Dropouts
Educational Operating Plan
 (EOP)
End-of-year checkout lists
Evaluations/action plans
Exams
Facilities
Facility requests
Faculty meetings
Family Life Education (FLE)
Federal impact aid cards
Field trips
Gangs (issues and preven-
 tion)
GED referrals
Graduation
Grants
Gross and simple negligence
Hall sweeps
Handbook (students and
 teacher)
Homebound services and
 referrals
Homecoming and related
 vents
Interviewing and hiring staff
Inventory

Leadership Team (staff and students)
Lunch blocks
Master schedule
Mental health situations
Mentoring and peer mentoring
Mission, vision statements, staff themes
Monthly administrator meetings
Observations (formal, informal, pop-ins)
Office of Civil Rights (OCR)
Parent disputes
Parking
Pep rallies
Police reports
Professional development
Professional organizations
Prom/after prom
PTSA and booster clubs
Recruiting and interviewing teachers
Remediation and enrichment programs
SACS/regional accreditation

SAT prep
School board meetings
School climate and culture
School finance
School law/due process
School resource officer (SRO)
School security cameras
Sexual harassment
Special education
Staff development
Student assistance plans
Student mediation/conflict resolution
Student obligations
Student teachers
Subs and sub finder
Supervision (school and extracurricular activities)
Surveys/questionnaires
Teacher recognition
Technology training
Testing (state testing)
Trespassers
Truancy/compulsory attendance
Volunteers

References

Collins J. (2001). *Good to great*. New York: Harper Collins Publishers.

Covey, S. R. (2004). *The 8th habit: From effectiveness to greatness*. New York: Free Press.

Friedman, T. (2005). *The world is flat: A brief history of the twenty-first century*. New York: Farrar, Straus, and Giroux.

Goertz, M., & Duffy, M. (2001). *Assessment and accountability across the 50 states* (Consortium for policy research in education, Policy Brief RB 33). Philadelphia: University of Pennsylvania.

Hess, F. M. (2003). *A license to lead? A new leadership agenda for America's schools*. Retrieved October 4, 2004, from http://www.ppionline.org/documents/NewLeadership0103.pdf

Learning To Give. (2008). *Learning to give*. Retrieved January 29, 2008, from http://www.learningtogive.org/search/quotes/Display_Quotes.asp?subject_id=51 search_type=subject

Maslow's Hierarchy. (2002–2007). *Maslow's hierarchy of needs*. Retrieved July 7, 2008, from http://www.netmba.com/mgmt/ob/motivation/maslow/

McGuire, M. Y. (2002). *The changing role of school leaders: Michigan leaders address the issue of principal certification*. Retrieved July 3, 2005, from http://www.cenmi.org/LeadingChange/W04/article2a.asp

MotivateUs.com (2008). *Motivation and inspiration on a daily basis.* Retrieved February 1, 2008, from http://www.motivateus.com

No child left behind act. (2001). Retrieved June 30, 2005, from http://www.ed.gov/nclb/landing.jtml

Popham, W. J. (2003). *Test better, teach better: The instructional role of assessment.* Alexandria, VA: Association for Supervision and Curriculum Development (ASCD).

Samuels, C. A. (2008). Managers help principals balance time. *Education Week, 27(23),* 1–2.

Schlechty, P. C. (2002). *Working on the work: An action plan for teachers, principals, and superintendents.* San Francisco, CA: Jossey Bass.

Schmoker, M. (2006). *Results now: How we can achieve unprecedented improvements in teaching and learning.* Alexandria, VA: Association for Supervision and Curriculum Development.

The History Place (2008). *The history place—Great speeches collection.* Retrieved October 21, 2008, from http://www.historyplace.com/speeches/jfk-inaug.htm

Tomlinson, C. A. (2003). Teaching all students. *Educational Leadership, 61(2),* 6–11.

Tomlinson, C. A., & Allan S. D. (2000). *Leadership for differentiating schools and classrooms.* Alexandria, VA: Association for Supervision and Curriculum Development.

Tressel, J. (2008). The winners manual for the game of life. Carol Stream, IL: Tyndale House.

Webster's ninth new collegiate dictionary. (1983). Springfield, MA: Merriam-Webster.

Zmuda, A. (2008). Springing into active learning. *Educational Leadership, 66(3),* 38–42.